Spitfires & Autogiros

A History of Upper Culham Farm, RAF Henley-on-Thames

Darren J. Pitcher

Published by
Robert Boyd Publications
260 Colwell Drive
Witney, Oxfordshire OX28 5LW

Printed and bound by
Information Press
Southfield Road
Eynsham, Oxford OX29 4JB

Distributed by
Darren J. Pitcher
11 Clarence Road
Henley-on-Thames
Oxfordshire RG9 2DP

First published 2010

ISBN: 978 1 899536 77 1

Title Page
Wartime aerial view of Henley, possibly from 1944 (Air Historical Branch via Ken Delve)

Photographs in the book are credited where known either by individual or from a collection, uncredited photographs have been loaned from individuals or collectors but their original source is unknown.

CONTENTS

INTRODUCTION

When I started out with the idea for doing this book little did I know where it would lead. I thought I knew all about my local wartime airfield, and thought that it wouldn't amount to much of a history, how wrong I was. The great thing about doing research is that there is so much information out there to discover and when looking for information on this particular subject I certainly found more than I could have imagined.

This airfield might not have been a famous fighter or bomber station but the part it played in it's short wartime existence like so many other similar airfields, from the important task of being a relief landing ground for the training of pilots for most of it's operational life, to the assembly of Photo Reconnaissance Spitfires built in garages in Reading, and the daily comings and goings of 529 (Rota) Squadron with it's autogiros and becoming the first RAF Squadron to use helicopters, albeit for a very short time.

When you look at the wider picture it's not just the history of a particular airfield but everything else that is connected with it and where it leads, in this case to the pilots who trained here going onto operational Squadrons, the Spitfires that flew vital photographic missions over Europe, and 529 Squadron doing important radar and anti-aircraft calibration work.

This airfield may have disappeared many years ago but it's important not to be forgotten, and I hope that the following pages will give a good account of it's varied history.

Darren J. Pitcher

ACKNOWLEDGEMENTS

The following have provided much of the information for this book, which would not have been possible without their help and the time they have afforded me. I would like to particularly thank my Father and Peter Arnold for information on the Spitfire histories, my Uncle for collecting so many books which have been a useful source of reference, Roger Austin for providing the airfield plan and deciphering the 529 Squadron operational records, David & Diana Painter for information on his Uncle's work at Vickers-Supermarine, Ken & Jean Fostekew at the Museum of Berkshire Aviation for access to their archives, Francis Hanford at the Trenchard Museum at Halton, Jim Waldron, Bob Sparrow, Douglas Rough, and everyone else who has contributed both information and photographs, I thank you all.

Peter Amos, Peter R Arnold, Roger Austin, Alf Blume, Phil Butler, Eddie Coates, Bob Cromwell, Peter Davis, Nigel Dawe & www.pixture.co.uk, Peter Delaney: Wargrave Local Historical Society, Ken Delve, Len Denton, Peter Durrant, Peter Elliott: Royal Air Force Museum, Hendon, Ken Ellis, Catherine Evans, Malcolm Fillmore, Peter Fitzmaurice, Vic Flintham, Ken & Jean Fostekew & the Museum of Berkshire Aviation, John & Frances Green, Francis Hanford: Trenchard Museum, RAF Halton, Edwin & Rachel Hayes, Lee Howard, Guy Jefferson, Allan Jerome, John Bernard Jones, Sven-Erik Jonsson: Swedish Aviation Historical Society Archive, Kevin Katzke, Peter Malone, Wojtek Matusiak, John MacMillan (friend of Johnnie Wakefield family), Steve McClean, Eloise Morton: The River and Rowing Museum, Henley, Michael Oakey, David & Diana Painter, John Pitcher, Robert Pitcher, Glyn Ramsden, Peter Randall, Richard Riding: RTR Collection, Robin Rigby, Douglas Rough, Dave Rushton, John Sargeant, John Sewell: Hunter Penrose Ltd, Robert Shaw, Bob Sparrow, Alan Taylor: South African Air Force Museum, Julian Temple, Kenneth Tilley, Tony Verey: Brakspears Pub Company, Jim & Vivienne Waldron, Dave Welch, Henley-on-Thames, Maidenhead & Reading Library Staff, The National Archive: Kew, Personal Plane Services, and all the contributors to the Henley Standard over the years.

BIBLIOGRAPHY

The following books have been a valuable reference, and are highly recommended reading

The Circus is in Town
Those Fabulous Flying Years - Colin Cruddas (Air-Britain) 2003

Spitfires from Garages
Above All Unseen - Edward Leaf (Patrick Stephens) 1997
Classic Warbirds Merlin PR Spitfires - Wojtek Matusiak (Ventura) 2007
Eyes For The Phoenix, Allied Aerial Photo-Reconnaissance Operations South East Asia 1941-45
Geoffrey J. Thomas (Hikoki) 1999
Forty Years On, A Spitfire Flies Again - Lettice Curtis (Nelson & Saunders) 1985
Photo Reconnaissance, The Operational History - Andrew J. Brooks (Ian Allan) 1975
Spitfire International - Helmut Terbeck, Harry van der Meer & Ray Sturtivant (Air Britain) 2002
Spitfire in Blue - Hugh Smallwood (Osprey Aerospace) (Reed Books Ltd) 1996
Spitfire The History - Eric B Morgan and Edward Shacklady (Key Publishing) Fifth Edition 2000
Spitfire, A Test Pilot's Story - Jeffrey Quill (Arrow Books) reprint 1986

529 (Rota) Squadron
British Service Helicopters, A Pictorial History - Richard Gardner & Reginald Longstaff (Hale) 1985
The Hoverfly File - Eric Myall (Air Britain) 1997
Radar - A Wartime Miracle, Colin Latham and Anne Stobbs (Alan Sutton Publishing Ltd) 1996

Local Wartime Accidents and Incidents
The Chiltern Prangs - R. Setter and P. Halliday (Chiltern Aircraft Research Group)
Bomber Command Losses 1943 & 1944 - W. R. Chorley (Midland Counties) 1996 & 1997

General
Fly and Deliver: A Ferry Pilot's Log Book, Hugh Bergel (Airlife) 1982
Aircraft of the Royal Air Force since 1918 (Ninth Edition) - Owen Thetford (Putnam) 1995
Military Airfields of Oxfordshire, Michael J. F. Bowyer (Patrick Stephens) 1988
Oxfordshire Airfields in the Second World War - Robin J. Brooks (Countryside Books) 2001
Royal Air Force Aircraft series, Military Aviation (Various Titles) - Air Britain (Historians)
The Military Airfields of Britain, Northern Home Counties - Ken Delve (Crowood) 2007
Thames Valley Airfields in the Second World War - Robin J. Brooks (Countryside Books) 2000
The Book of Wargrave, The First Edition 1986 reprinted 1987
Wings Over Woodley - Julian C Temple (Aston) 1987
Miles Aircraft, The Early Years - Peter Amos (Air Britain) 2009
First Landing, The story of the first arrival of aircraft on the Halton Estate - Francis Hanford
(Trenchard Museum Publication)
Plus the following periodicals:
Aeroplane Monthly, Air Enthusiast, Aviation News, Flypast, Wingspan,
and not forgetting the Henley Standard and Maidenhead Advertiser

UPPER CULHAM FARM, CRAZIES HILL

Crazies Hill is a small hamlet situated to the east of Henley-on-Thames, Oxfordshire and next to Cockpole Green in the civil parish of Wargrave, Berkshire. The name 'Crazies Hill' derives from a well, the only source of clean drinking water on the hill. It was known in the Celtic language as Cray-wy-zeath Hill, that is the hill of 'the fresh clean water of the waterless place.' The source of the well was a muddy spring in the local woods known as Rebra's Well but also known by the locals as Rebecca's Well. In 1870 the then Curate of Wargrave, the Reverend Granville Phillimore and his parishioners raised enough money to install a proper basin and later raised a further £25 to have a proper brick surround built. Other variations on the name derive from the poppy and buttercup which were often called a 'crazies' many of which grew on the hill. Cockpole Green's name derives also from the Celtic as Cog-Pabell Gre Eyn, which translates as the little green at the crossroads.

The land at Upper Culham Farm 2½ miles north of Wargrave belonged to a Colonel Henry Andrew Micklem, the son of Major General Edward Micklem who had a house at nearby Rosehill. He tenanted the land out to a local family, the Prings during 1924, they also ran nearby Goulders Farm, which is still run today by the Hayes family on one half of the old airfield. When Vera Pring got married they used the field for setting off on honeymoon to the Channel Islands on the 15th May 1935, flying out in a de Havilland Leopard Moth to Southsea, the plane returned later to give flights to some of the guests. The field also played host to a visit from Alan Cobham in 1935 and used for Henley agricultural shows during 1936-39, 1949 and 1957-59.

The responsibility of choosing sites as potential airfields lay with the Air Ministry Aerodrome Board. The method of finding suitable sites consisted of studying Ordnance Survey maps looking for suitable flat areas of land that were free from obstructions, also it was important to ascertain the nature of subsoil for the area, in the case of Upper Culham Farm consisting of chalk and flint, the soil of the area being made up of clay and loam, the chief crops grown in the area at the time were Wheat, Barley and Oats. The area chosen was then inspected on foot by walking around the proposed site, and if found suitable, the owner would receive a form of requisition from the Secretary of State under the defence regulations of 1939 giving them authority to take possession of the land, certifying that it would be suitable to use. Land owners of the farms were normally paid compensation for loss of crops and income by the Air Ministry.

The work to clear the land and make a suitable landing ground at Upper Culham Farm started in late 1939 and continued through the harsh winter of 1940. The local area was covered by Elm trees and most of these were felled, and a sunken track which ran across the field known as Anniper Lane had to be filled in to level it off. A small line of trees running partly along the track had to be cleared, then grass needed to be sown, but an area covering roughly 150 acres was eventually created.

A view taken in November 2009 of part of the former airfield looking north with Upper Culham Lane and the White Cottages on the left and in the centre distance Upper Culham Farm. (DJP)

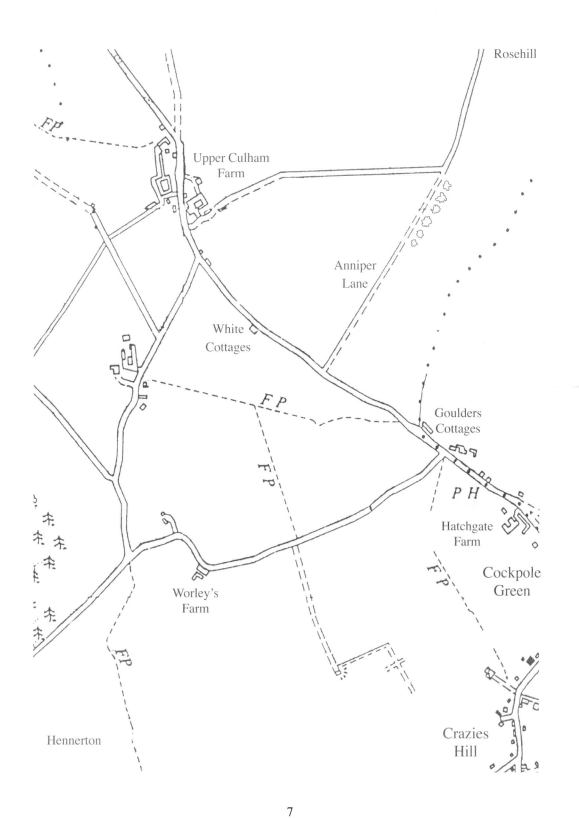

EARLY AVIATION

Henley-on-Thames situated on the edge of the Chiltern Hills in Oxfordshire is associated mostly with it's links to rowing, the first Oxford and Cambridge University boat race was held here in 1829, and the first of the world famous Regattas was held in June 1839 and have been held ever since. One of the first Henley-on-Thames aviation related stories is connected with these events and concerns Douglas Graham Gilmour who on 7th July 1911 delighted the crowds at that years Royal Regatta. Over the regatta he would swoop in from behind Sham Hill in his Bristol Boxkite before flying up to Marsh Lock and then turning and flying back down the length of the course, his landing wheels dipping in and out of the water, before landing to much applause in a field behind Sham Hill, he might well have used Upper Culham Farm although this has not been proven. He departed later to Brooklands, Surrey. As daring and dangerous as this sounds however it was not shared by the Royal Aero Club who suspended his licence for a month for endangering public safety, from the 18th July. Later exploits involved dive-bombing the Oxford and Cambridge teams during the Boat Race of 1911 and also flying under Tower Bridge. To underline the war potentialities of the air, he loaded his aeroplane with oranges and "bombed" the forts of Portsmouth and ships of the fleet there. In 1910 he had purchased a Bleriot aeroplane in France which would have cost about £480, he then flew it back across the Channel. On the morning of the 17th February 1912 he was testing a new monoplane on a flight from Brooklands when it suffered structural failure and crashed in Richmond Park, London, sadly he was killed in this accident becoming the tenth aviator to die in the United Kingdom since powered flight began.

Douglas Graham Gilmour
(Catherine Evans)

A Bristol Boxkite Replica based with the Shuttleworth
Trust at Old Warden in Bedfordshire (DJP)

During the days of September 1913 army manoeuvres of the Household Divisions were being carried out partly to gain experience in moving an army using motor vehicles, and to see if a main road could cope with such traffic, the task being to gather forces together near Aylesbury, Buckinghamshire where exercises would take place. Aircraft were to play a supporting role in these exercises which were divided into two armies, the "Whiteland" and "Brownland". The Royal Flying Corps provided three Squadrons Nos. 3, 4 and 5 with 3 Squadron supporting the "Brownland" forces. In charge of 3 Squadron at Netheravon, Wiltshire was Major Robert Brooke-Popham who had to locate suitable landing grounds on the planned route. Brooke-Popham would travel to each landing site location by a hired taxi to command the use of the owners land. The aircraft departed on the 12th with the "Whiteland" aircraft of 4 and 5 Squadrons "C" Flight with Bleriot aircraft using sites at Hungerford, Wantage and Oxford and the "Brownland" aircraft of 3 Squadron "A" and "B" Flights which consisted of Royal Aircraft Factory BE.2a, BE.3 and BE.4 as well as Henry-Farman F20 pusher biplanes types using Farnborough, Haines Hill near Twyford, and Rosehill near Henley-on-Thames.

The Rosehill site belonged to Major General Edward Micklem, who would probably have been known by Major Brooke-Popham and would have given him the permission to use the land, which would have been one of the fields at Upper Culham Farm as this is the only suitable site in the area for landings and is next to Rosehill, the criteria being that the landing area be 200 yards square and free of stones and ridges. On the 18th September sometime after 11.00 a.m. the aircraft of 3 Squadron arrived at Rosehill but no further flying took place that day. The 19th of September brought foggy conditions to the area something that they had suffered with since the exercises began although conditions improved during the afternoon and one plane the BE.3 made a reconnaissance flight and dropped a message bag by parachute at nearby Culham Court. The final destination for the exercises was Halton, Buckinghamshire where a landing area had been created using a field on Halton Park belonging to the estate of the Rothschilds. The first ever aircraft to land at Halton arrived on the 18th September with the rest following over the next two days. The exercises took place over the following days with aircraft from both forces doing mock battle and reconnaissance flights in the local area, two airships were also used the Delta and Eta from 1 Squadron, these for observation of the ground forces, 3 Squadron engaging these in combat. In fact 3 Squadron which had been formed at Larkhill from 2 Company (Heavier-than-air) Air Battalion, Royal Engineers on the 13th May 1912 had become the first to use heavier than air machines with the motto Tertius primus erit, meaning "The third shall be the first".

Aircraft, pilots and observers used by 3 Squadron "A" and "B" Flights

Captain Allen, Flt Cdr	"A"	BE.4	No.204
Captain Picton-Warlow	"A"	BE Experimental	
Lieutenant Abercromby	"A"	BE Experimental	
Lieutenant Porter	"A"	BE.3	No.203
Lieutenant Lawrence	"A"	BE.2a	No.226 on loan from 5 Squadron
flew with Major Brooke-Popham as observer			
Captain Herbert, Flt Cdr	"B"	Farman F20	
Lieutenant Cholmonderley	"B"	Farman F20	
Lieutenant Hubbard	"B"	Farman F20	
Lieutenant Stopford	"B"	Farman F20	No.351
Lieutenant Shekelton	"B"	Farman F20	
Lieutenant Adams	"B"	Farman F20	on loan from 5 Squadron
Lieutenant Birch	"B"	Farman F20	on loan from 5 Squadron

Although the aircraft of 3 Squadron stayed at the site of Rosehill for just one day and night and then left for Halton, ironically thirty-one years later almost to the month aircraft from Halton would be coming the other way with the arrival at Henley of 529 (Rota) Squadron the final military users of the site.

Royal Aircraft Factory BE.2a No.226 used by 3 Squadron on loan during September 1913

THE CIRCUS IS IN TOWN

Part of the site at Upper Culham Farm, between the farm and Anniper Lane was used on the 19th June 1935 by Sir Alan Cobham who chose it as the venue for one of his National Aviation Display tours that visited hundreds of towns and cities throughout the country, some of them regular airfields and some just fields cleared for the occasion. It gave the fare-paying public the chance to experience flights in different types of aircraft, including the Airspeed Ferry ten-seat biplane, specially designed by Alan Cobham who was one of the founding directors of the Airspeed company. A display was put on twice a day and pilots and their aircraft would perform various daring stunts and aerobatics in front of the crowds, such as obstacle races, wing-walking, aerobatics, crazy flying and parachute jumps.

SIR ALAN COBHAM'S
GREAT NEW
AIR DISPLAY
BRITAIN'S FINEST PILOTS
IN AN ENTIRELY *NEW* PROGRAMME.

FLIGHT LIEUT. TYSON
Supreme Display Pilot, in amazing new feats.

LOOPING TIED TOGETHER
A superb display of close formation flying.

THE "WINGLESS" AUTOGIRO
The most, extraordinary aircraft in existence.

HIGH SPEED AEROBATICS
More thrilling than ever.

MR IVOR PRICE and MISS NAOMI HERON-MAXWELL
Britain's leading parachutists, in DUAL PULL OFF PARACHUTE DESCENTS

MISS JOAN MEAKIN
The only girl performing Aerobatics in a Glider.

OBSTACLE AIR RACE

PASSENGER FLIGHTS
In Ten Aircraft, Newest and best.

Humorous Events, Crazy Flying, Free Flight Competitions, etc.

20 BRILLIANT NEW EVENTS
Including Personal Appearance of MR. C. A. W. SCOTT, Winner of Australia Air Race.

UPPER CULHAM, HENLEY (Maidenhead Road), WEDNESDAY, JUNE 19th,

Continuous 2.30pm, till Dusk. Two Complete Displays 2.30 and 6.40 p.m.

Special Children's Hour 5.30 to 6.30 p.m.

ADMISSION 1/3. CHILDREN 5d. CARS 1/- FLIGHTS from 4/-

A reproduced advertisement featured in the Henley Standard of June 14th 1935

Aircraft used on the 1935 National Aviation Display Tour included the following

Airspeed Ferry G-ABSI, Avro 504N G-ACLV, G-ACOD, G-ACPV, G-ADBD
Avro Tutor G-ABZP, Avro Cadet G-ACLU, G-ACOZ, G-ACPB
Cierva C30 Autogiro G-ACYH (later used by the RAF as DR622 of 529 (Rota) Squadron)
de Havilland Tiger Moth G-ACEZ, Handley-Page Clive G-ABYX, Westland Wessex G-ADFZ

SIR ALAN COBHAM'S AIR DISPLAY.
GLIDING AND PARACHUTING.

MISS JOAN MEAKIN (the Famous Glider Girl)

Miss Joan Meakin, the celebrated "glider girl" was once described as the "pied piper" of flying. This year again she is calling on the nation's youth to follow her into the air. At 21 years of age she is equally accomplished and is probably the most experienced woman glider pilot in the world. She established a long-distance record for women with a glide of 52 miles from Bristol to Salisbury and she is the only woman who has ever looped a glider. On one occasion she looped her glider 20 consecutive times. "Gliding' is so inexpensive that it should be brought within the reach of everyone," says Miss Meakin. " A gliding club should be formed at every town in the country, and every boy or girl who wishes to learn to glide should have the chance of doing so, exactly as they do in Germany. It is a marvellous sport and is the best possible training for a flying career." To enable her to describe her demonstration , Miss Meakin has had a specially designed wireless transmitter fitted to her new "Wolf" sailplane, and her voice is relayed to the spectators through the display loudspeakers. Her machine is the first engine less aircraft ever fitted with wireless. She will be towed behind an aeroplane up to height of about 1,500 feet, and during her glide to earth will give an exhibition of gliding aerobatics.

An Added Attraction.

The demonstration of the new "direct control" Autogiro at Sir Alan Cobham's Display will be the first public exhibition of this wonderful new invention in the Maidenhead and Henley districts. This new Autogiro has been described as the "wingless wonder" since it dispenses entirely with any kind of movable control surface. It has no elevators, rudders or ailerons. The pilot's sole control is a "joy-stick" connected to the shaft carrying the revolving "rotor." He steers the machine, banks it on turns, and causes it to climb or descend by inclining the "rotor." In other respects besides control, the new Autogiro claims to be a great improvement on any other aircraft in existence.

Owing to its ability to fly slowly and hover in the air practically stationary it has been adopted by the London Police and has been used for control of road traffic. It can fly at considerably less than 30 m.p.h. so beware of the "Sky Traffic Cop." Sir Alan Cobham's Autogiro is equipped with wireless exactly similar to the Police Autogiros, and its pilot will give a complete demonstration of its extraordinary capabilities under orders transmitted by wireless from the ground.

The voice of the announcer speaking to the pilot will be relayed to the spectators through the Display loudspeakers and every evolution of the machine will be clearly explained by the pilot. Mr. R. J. Ashley, who will fly the machine in this special demonstration, is an Autogiro enthusiast who proved to be one of the best pupils of the Autogiro School at Hanworth Aerodrome, Middlesex, and actually makes the machine dance to music broadcast from the ground.

Passengers are promised a thrilling Air Cruise over the Thames Valley in Sir Alan Cobham's giant "Astra" air liner. This giant aeroplane carries 22 passengers in a spacious cabin. Each passenger has an armchair and a separate side-window, affording a magnificent view of the countryside. With two powerful Bristol "Jupiter" engines developing 1,100 h.p., the "Astra" will carry the air guests on a memorable cruise at 100 miles an hour in perfect safety and comfort. Their pilot will be Flight Lieutenant H. C. Johnson, the chief pilot of Sir Alan Cobham's display, who holds the amazing record of having taken up more than 140,000 people without mishap. The most nervous of passengers will forget their timidity in his hands.

The following is a report featured in the Henley Standard for June 21st 1935.

SIR ALAN COBHAM'S AIR DISPLAY.
WONDERFUL FLYING AT CULHAM FARM.

Sir Alan Cobham's famous air display paid its eagerly awaited visit to Henley and district on Wednesday last, a large field admirably suited for the purpose at Culham Farm, in the occupation of Mr. T. Pring being used as the flying ground.

Here quite a large crowd attended and witnessed a display fully in keeping with the high standard set by the "circus" in its visits to some 700 towns, in the course of which some half a million passengers have taken flights and 1,700,000 miles have been travelled in the air.

Everyone attending had the opportunity of taking a flight over the town of Henley and surrounding country in one or other of the several aircraft and the Airspeed "Ferry," capable of seating a dozen or more passengers and flown by Captain J. R. King, who has the unique distinction of having carried a quarter of a million passengers without mishap, proved very popular for this purpose. It was in this machine that the lucky winners of our free flight tickets flew. In addition, passengers were taken up in the smaller aeroplanes, and some of them even experienced the thrills of looping the loop and other stunts.

From the opening of the display at 2.30 until dusk there was hardly a dull moment. The aeroplanes were often flying very low and sometimes were only a few feet over the heads of the people assembled to watch the display. Everything was well organised, however, and no mishap of any sort occurred.

The chief stunter of the afternoon was Flight-Lieut. Geoffrey Tyson, who gave a remarkable display which included inverted flying, looping, rolling, etc and also picking up a small flag from the ground with a dagger attached to one of the tips of his machine. He was well backed up by other pilots taking part in a variety of other events. A very graceful display of soaring in a glider was given in faultless style by Miss Joan Meakin the "Glider girl," who was towed by aeroplane from Germany to England, and she showed wonderful control in a machine (if an engine less craft can be called a machine) that was appropriately described as "exquisite."

Miss Meakin's female companion in the display - Miss Naomi Heron-Maxwell, the "parachute girl" - was absent owing to her having to be in Germany to take a gliding course and her place was taken by Mr. A. L. Harris. Owing to the low clouds, however a parachute descent could not be included in the programme.

The wingless autogiro arrived during the course of the afternoon having flown from Rochester in a very short time. This unique machine attracted considerable attention and the clever piloting of it by Mr. T. Bulmore proved a revelation to all who saw it.

The attendance in the evening was not so great as would have been the case had the weather kept really fine, but the afternoon's programme was gone through again and thoroughly enjoyed, particularly the "bombing" with bags of flour a car that drove on to the arena. This car caught fire but the flames were speedily put out with extinguishers.

During the course of the afternoon and evening free flight competitions were run in connection with Messrs. Everest and Sheldrake's Ford motor display and Messrs. Hammants' C.A.V. and G.E.C. tent.

Free Flight Winners.

The winners of the free flights in connection with the offer made by Messrs. Everest and Sheldrake and the Ford Motor Company, were as follows:- Miss L. Newbury, Duke Street, Henley : Mr. T. M. Mills, Caxton Terrace, Henley : Mr. K. M. Horswell, St.Marks Road, Henley : Mr. F. Rolfe, Station Garage, Henley : Mr. N. Matthews, Bell Street, Henley : Mrs. Robson, Friday Street, Henley. Over eighty applications were received for the flights.

A Passenger's Impression

A passenger who went on one of the flights in the Airspeed "Ferry," writes as follows:-

I have never won a competition before, but I was fortunate enough to gain a free ticket at the Henley Cinema which enabled me to have a flight in one of the machines belonging to Sir Alan Cobham's air circus. I was of course very pleased about this and went over to Culham Farm on Wednesday, in high anticipation of a great event in my life. There surely can be no better feeling, than that of flying. The pilot yells contact, mechanics, who, in their turn, "swing the prop," and the triple engines burst into life.

The pilot looks to see which way the wind is blowing and sets his nose into the wind and "takes off." This is done to prevent "stalling," for if the joy stick is pulled back rapidly, the plane will drop some twenty feet before responding, and the danger of this is intensified if there is a tail wind, and the result disastrous if the plane is near the ground. Once off the ground the plane climbed slowly and soon the river in the shape of a small stream was just below us. Far away to the left could be seen Reading and the fields were like a patch work quilt, and the houses like doll's houses.

It was possible to see the Henley Grammar School, Westfield House and Friar Park but the flight was rather spoilt by the misty weather. Along the Fair Mile, cars were making use of their speed to show appreciation of the lifting of the 30 m.p.h. limit, the clouds forced us down rather low; their altitude was about 750 feet and our own about 500 feet. There were numbers of air pockets and from time to time the plane would lurch on her side, or drop some twenty feet in these air pockets. We were in the air for about ten minutes, and I had gained during that time impressions which it will not be easy to forget, and if other people have felt the same the air circus will have been much more than just an afternoon's entertainment.

I was most impressed by the speed and the short time which it took to cover the distance, we were about three minutes from Shiplake to Henley, and as I heard it remarked afterwards, it doesn't seem much up there, but when you come to walk it, well that's different and this remark sums up the whole significance of the display.

If it has provided an afternoon's amusement only its importance is negligible, but if it has aroused the enthusiasm of local people, and the belief in the safety and speed of air travel, its main object has been achieved, and air travel may become a significant factor in the organisation and commercial development of the country.

The Airspeed Ferry G-ABSI as used by Sir Alan Cobham's Flying Circus. Sir Alan John Cobham was born in May 1894 and was an English aviation pioneer. A member of the Royal Flying Corps in World War I . After the war he became a test pilot for the de Havilland aircraft company. In 1932 he started the National Aviation Day displays. Early experiments with in-flight refuelling resulted in a non-stop flight from London to India, using in-flight refuelling to extend the plane's flight duration.
The photograph was taken at a show held near Maidenhead (Maidenhead Advertiser)

Some of the aircraft used by Sir Alan Cobhams National Aviation Tours 1935

Avro 504N G-ACLV ex RAF J8673
Which was destroyed in a collision with
G-ACPD at Claybury in April 1937.
(Charles Holland Collection via Ken Tilley)

Avro 504N G-ACOD ex RAF F8713
Which was destroyed in a collision with
G-ADFZ over Blackpool in September 1935.
(Charles Holland Collection via Ken Tilley)

Avro 504N G-ADBD ex RAF K1245
Crashed at Southend in July 1936.
(Charles Holland Collection via Ken Tilley)

Avro 621 Tutor G-ABZP
flown by Geoffrey Tyson.
The aircraft was scrapped in 1940.
(Charles Holland Collection via Ken Tilley)

Avro 640 Cadet G-ACPB
destroyed by fire at Croydon in 1940.
(Charles Holland Collection via Ken Tilley)

de Havilland DH82 Tiger Moth G-ACEZ
This particular Tiger Moth had been flown
inverted by Geoffrey Tyson across the
English Channel in July 1934.
Crashed at Andover in August 1961.
(David Gray via Ken Tilley)

Westland Wessex G-ADFZ
a six seater light Transport.
(Charles Holland Collection via Ken Tilley)

Avro 671 Rota G-ACYH
This was later impressed into RAF service
with 529 (Rota) Squadron as DR622.
(picture supplied by Kevin Katzke)

Handley-Page Clive G-ABYX "Astra"
22 seat passenger airliner ex RAF J9126
Scrapped during 1935.
(Charles Holland Collection via Ken Tilley)

ONE DAY ONLY.
MONDAY. 10 MAY
HENLEY-ON-THAMES
UPPER CULHAM FARM, WARGRAVE
Continuous 2 Displays 2.15 till Dusk. Popular Prices.
FREQUENT BUSES FROM ALL PARTS.

GREAT AIR DISPLAYS VISIT.
ONE DAY SHOW AT UPPER CULHAM FARM.

On Monday 10th May 1937, at Upper Culham Farm, Henley, will be presented an air display organised by men and pilots who have gauged the public likes and requirements as regards entertainment and instructional value to a nicety. This air show will provide a unique opportunity for all to see an up-to-date exhibition of superb airman ship in amazing machines specially designed for this class of work, by air pilots chosen for their skill and daring.

The show is designed to interest everyone of all ages and will consist of two displays lasting from 2.15 p.m. to dusk. Machines from the 10 seater airliner to fast single seaters will be on view and one few opportunities of flying Henley people will be available.

The pilots are all trained men and picked because of their unique aeronautical knowledge. Among them is E. W. ("Jock") Bonar M.B.E. Flying since 1932, he has carried over 100,000 passengers in the British Isles alone, mostly in aerobatic flights. He was a member of the famous 25 Fighter Squadron when he made the first combined aerobatic display at Hendon, and was co-pilot with Colonel J. C. Fitzmaurice in the Mildenhall-Australia air race when they flew the Bellanca machine "The Irish Swoop."

Britain's Bird Man

He is only one of the pilots, but love of the spectacular will focus attention on a pilot of a different kind. This, of course is Mr. Harry Ward, Britain's first and only "Bird Man." The "Bird Man" launches himself into space from an aeroplane and the spectators are treated to the superb spectacle of a man performing swallow like swoops and glides. On descending to a certain level, he closes his wings to his side and his parachute brings him safely to earth. On the first occasion he made a flight of this kind Mr. Ward covered three miles in a straight glide before performing loops and spins.

RELIEF LANDING GROUND

After Sir Alan Cobhams National Aviation Tour had used Upper Culham Farm in 1935, certain sites he had visited on his tours were often considered as suitable airfields by the Air Ministry and this was the case with Upper Culham Farm. The Royal Air Force under the control of Flying Training Command decided that the field could be made into a Relief Landing Ground (RLG). The work to clear and remove the trees had been completed by early to mid 1940, and after the land had been levelled off a suitable 700-800 yard grass area was created as a landing site, the work being carried out by the firm British Runways Ltd. Metal tracking was laid down to stop the surface breaking up in bad weather. In what was essentially just an empty field the RAF established themselves here with a few huts in the north-western corner of the field but not much else in the way of infrastructure, although more buildings were added throughout it's wartime use.

(DJP)

13 Elementary Flying Training School

On the 4th July 1940 the de Havilland Tiger Moths of 13 Elementary Flying Training School (EFTS) 'A' Flight based at nearby White Waltham started to make use of the field. This unit had been a civilian run operation before the war operated by the de Havilland School of Flying and was taken over by the Air Ministry, although still run as a civilian outfit. The school was formed in accordance with Air Ministry instructions to carry out ab initio training for pupil pilots of the Royal Air Force and elementary and advanced training for Officers and NCO's of the R.A.F.O. and R.A.F.V.R. The aircraft would fly over to the field daily and use it for training practice, mainly take-offs and landings known as circuits and bumps, firstly during daytime and then also at night from August 1940 onwards. With an obvious need to train more pilots this relieved the pressure from what was a very congested airfield, for as well as training, White Waltham was also the home of the Air Transport Auxiliary (ATA) a civilian organisation which ferried aircraft around the country. 13 EFTS made use of Henley up until 20th December 1940 when they moved from White Waltham due to airfield congestion, lack of adequate offices and disciplinary difficulties to Westwood near Peterborough.

Pilot Training

The first stage of pilot training was to join an Elementary Flying Training School (EFTS), here the pupil is introduced to the operations of the aircraft, usually in a de Havilland Tiger Moth or Miles Magister. These were dual control to allow both pupil and instructor to be in charge of the aircraft at any one time. The pupil would have to be pass an ab initio course of up to fifty hours before any further training. This would usually involve endless circuits of take-offs and landings. Generally it was regarded that a pilot should be able to fly solo within ten hours although this obviously varied slightly from pupil-to-pupil although anyone who took over sixteen hours was considered not to be worth persevering with. Blind flying will also be introduced at a later stage, the cockpit in which the pupil sits is covered with a hood, this is to simulate flying in bad visibility and weather, and also to teach flying by using just the instruments alone. Aerobatics and practice force-landings also became part of the pilot's training.

Instructors for 13 EFTS

The Following is taken from (AIR 29/618) from The National Archives, Kew
13 Elementary Flying Training School, July-December 1940

Flying Instructors -	W/Cdr G. C. O'Donnell	(R.A.F.)
	S/L R. W. Reeve	(R.A.F.O.)
	S/L G. M. Cox	(R.A.F.O.)
	F/Lt G. N. P. Stringer	(R.A.F.O.)
	F/Lt A. J. Hicks	(R.A.F.O.)
	F/Lt D. A. Rea	(R.A.F.O.)
	F/Lt C. H. N. L'Estrange	(R.A.F.V.R.)
	F/O C. D. Beaumont	(R.A.F.O.)
	F/Lt T. E. Wesson	(R.A.F.O.)
	F/Lt J. O. H. Lobley	(R.A.F.O.)
	F/Lt B. P. A. Vallance	(R.A.F.O.)
	F/Lt R. L. Bowes	(R.A.F.V.R.)
	F/O R. Findlay	(R.A.F.O.)
	F/O Baron D. R. B. de Sarigny	(R.A.F.O.)
	F/Lt P. C. Horden	(R.A.F.V.R.)
	F/Lt J. D. Wood	(R.A.F.V.R.)
	F/Lt W. B. Thompson	(R.A.F.V.R.)
	P/O W. M. Mackay	(R.A.F.V.R.)
	F/O J. W. R. Kempe	(R.A.F.V.R.)
	F/O G. P. Butcher	(R.A.F.O.)
	P/O H. Arnott	(R.A.F.V.R.)
	F/Lt R. S. Munday	(R.A.F.O.)
	F/Lt D. R. Keiller	(R.A.F.O.)
	F/Lt A. C. Mills	(R.A.F.O.)
	P/O A. F. P. Fane	(R.A.F.V.R.)
	P/O G. C. R. Moody	
	F/O K. W. Hole	
	Sgt P. C. Sawyer	
	Sgt J. F. Schofield	
	Sgt R. J. Shuttlebotham	
	Sgt Jack. P. Smith	
	Sgt S. A. L. Tarlton	
Ground Instructors -	Mr. L. S. T. Brown, Chief Ground Instructor	
	Mr. T. H. Catley, Armament Instructor	
	Mr. F. J. Preston, Assistant Armament Instructor	
	Mr. A. R. Stevens, Navigation Instructor	
	Mr. W. E. Doughty, Photographic Instructor	

There were eight courses carried out whilst 13 EFTS were using Henley, the first commencing on 25th July 1940 with 60 LAC this was completed by 7th September. The final course finishing by 18th December. Courses generally lasted for five weeks to seven weeks The total amount of pilots trained during this period amounted to over 400 these included Officers and NCO's from Belgium although not all of them were successful and many were rejected. The average hours flown during the period were 44 hours and 17 minutes. The average examination result being 79.3%.

8 Elementary Flying Training School

Control of the airfield was taken over on the 3rd February 1941 by the Woodley based 8 Elementary Flying Training School (EFTS), this school had been upgraded to a 'B' type establishment and was operated by Phillips & Powis Ltd, and came under the control of 50 Group, Flying Training Command. Consisting of around fifty-four aircraft and ninety pupils, they had planned to use Sheffield Farm at Theale as an RLG but this field was not ready and use of this was transferred to use by 26 EFTS so 8 EFTS used Henley as a Relief Landing Ground, this time with the Miles Magister trainer and a small number of Tiger Moths. The aircrew were conveyed to Henley each morning, afternoon and evening from Woodley, as they were housed at Sandford Manor near Woodley. From the 2nd September 1941 night flying was introduced here for training of "ab initio" instruction course pupils. In accordance with the Headquarters of Flying Training Command instructions, the Air Ministry decided that the airfield needed upgrading and so contractors erected three blister hangars and several smaller huts including a domestic site with accommodation for 270 personnel. With buildings now available aircraft could be left here overnight with the ground-crew also being able to stay. When the majority of training pilots was transferred to overseas, 8 EFTS was disbanded on the 21st September 1942 although one grading flight was retained at Henley.

A field situated between Woodley and White Waltham near the village of Waltham St.Lawrence, Berkshire was allocated as an Emergency Landing Ground (ELG) for use by 13 EFTS and later used by 8 EFTS and 10 FIS.

Miles Magister N3788 represents the type used by 8 EFTS, seen at Old Warden Military Airshow in August 2009 in pre-war yellow training colours. (DJP)

Allan Jerome who worked for Phillips & Powis at Woodley remembers having to rebuild a Miles Magister at Henley by fitting a whole new centre section to the aircraft after a particularly heavy landing one day, the work taking about a week to achieve. He also remembers a USAAF Douglas Dakota, whose pilot after noticing Tiger Moth's doing circuits landed to see if he could get a flight in one, he did and then returned the favour by giving the workers a flight in the Dakota, including the guard from the entrance gate guardhouse.

Allan Jerome pictured beside a Miles Magister at the Museum of Berkshire Aviation at Woodley, Berkshire. (DJP)

10 Flying Instructors School (Elementary)

It is uncertain when the 10 Flying Instructors School (FIS) first made use of Henley as an RLG, the school was formed on the 22nd July 1942 and may have continued to use the airfield from this date. The school had the task of teaching selected pilots as instructors for EFTS units both at home and abroad, taking over the task from 8 EFTS after that had been disbanded and was based at Woodley, Berkshire, using the de Havilland Tiger Moth and the Miles Magister, as well as the more advanced and powerful Miles Master I and II. At its height they had nearly 100 training aircraft including sixty-eight Tiger Moths.

The Flying Instructors School was disbanded at Woodley in May 1946 becoming part of the Central Flying School, although two flights did remain at Woodley and reverted back to being known as 8 EFTS. The unit was later renamed as 8 Reserve Flying Training School in March 1947.

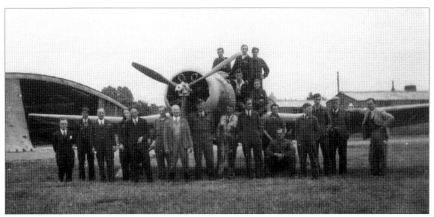

Ground crew with a Miles Master II of 10 Flying Instructors School at Henley, Miles employee Peter Weller is standing on the wing, third right, many locals were employed as ground crew. The photograph was taken outside a blister hangar
(see Airfield layout location 15) (C. H. Thomas Collection)

Night Flying

Night flying at an RLG involved using floodlighting and lights known as Glim lights, these were white and red and yellow in colour, red lights marked the areas where there were obstructions and yellow marked the area of the safe landing run. Gooseneck lamps, which were parraffin lights were lit in any misty or hazy conditions. A Chance floodlight would illuminate the runway and there was a "T" shape illumination to indicate the wind direction. Lit up taxying posts showed the area of the flarepath.

Wargrave Air Cadets

Wargrave Piggot School had a detachment of the Air Cadets which had been given an old Westland built aeroplane either a Wallace or Wapiti that had no wings attached, however this did not deter them from finding out that some fuel had been left in the tank. They managed to get the engine started then taxied the wingless aircraft around the school playing field.

Cadets from 447 ATC Squadron, Henley and probably Wargrave also had regular experience flights on sunday mornings in some of the training aircraft based at Henley.

The school was also registered by the Met. Office of the Air Ministry as Climatological Station 782/2/1 for the teaching of weather related subjects and did weather reports for the Met. Office relating to the area.

Aircraft used by Flying Training Units between 1940-1944

13 Elementary Flying Training School, White Waltham 1940
8 Elementary Flying Training School, Woodley from 1941-1942
10 Flying Instructors School, Woodley from ? - 1944

de Havilland Tiger Moth

L6922	10 FIS	to Maintenance Command airframe as 4464M 1-44
L6925	13 EFTS	Crashed 14-9-40, repaired
L6930	13 EFTS	Crashed 19-9-40, repaired
N6522	8 EFTS, 10 FIS	
N6539	10 FIS	
N6616	13 EFTS	
N6652	8 EFTS, 10 FIS	
N6667	13 EFTS	
N6669	13 EFTS	
N6674	13 EFTS	
N6725	8 EFTS	
N6737	8 EFTS	
N6774	8 EFTS	
N6776	10 FIS	
N6787	13 EFTS	
N6788	10 FIS	Crashed during low flying near Compton Beauchamp, Berkshire 7-6-43
N6789	13 EFTS	
N6790	13 EFTS	
N6791	13 EFTS	
N6793	13 EFTS	
N6795	13 EFTS	
N6796	13 EFTS	Struck telephone wires and crashed on overshoot at White Waltham, Berkshire 13-7-40
N6858	10 FIS	
N6925	10 FIS	
N9177	10 FIS	Struck Off Charge 14-7-44
N9204	13 EFTS	
N9241	10 FIS	
N9275	13 EFTS	Crashed 26-9-40, to de Havilland for repair
N9302	13 EFTS	
N9314	13 EFTS	
N9319	13 EFTS	Hit trees in a practice forced landing and crashed into a swamp near Petworth, Sussex 11-12-40
N9322	13 EFTS	
N9335	10 FIS	
N9347	10 FIS	
N9450	13 EFTS	Crashed inverted at Shiplake whilst doing aerobatics 28-7-40 LAC William. R. Driscoll and Instructor Sgt Jack. P. Smith were both killed
R4753	10 FIS	Struck Off Charge 14-7-44
R4758	8 EFTS	
R4762	13 EFTS	Crashed 23-8-40, repaired
R4768	13 EFTS	
R4770	10 FIS	
R4778	13 EFTS	Crashed Hawthorn Hill Racecourse, Berkshire 10-7-40 to DH for repair
R4834	13 EFTS	
R4849	13 EFTS	
R4857	13 EFTS	Spun into the ground near Twyford, Berkshire 30-8-40
R4877	13 EFTS	Crashed 28-10-40, repaired
R4924	10 FIS	
R4941	13 EFTS	

R4955	13 EFTS	
R4963	13 EFTS	
R4966	13 EFTS	
R5059	13 EFTS	
R5081	13 EFTS	
R5084	13 EFTS	
R5086	13 EFTS	
R5100	13 EFTS	
R5101	13 EFTS	
R5102	13 EFTS	Crashed 21-8-40, repaired
R5103	13 EFTS	
R5105	13 EFTS	
R5106	13 EFTS	Damaged and to de Havilland for repair 24-7-40
R5138	13 EFTS	
R5139	13 EFTS	
R5142	13 EFTS	
R5144	13 EFTS	
R5145	13 EFTS	
R5147	13 EFTS	
R5175	13 EFTS	
R5216	10 FIS	
T5362	13 EFTS	
T5363	13 EFTS	
T5365	13 EFTS	
T5366	13 EFTS	
T5367	13 EFTS	
T5368	13 EFTS	Crashed 7-12-40, to 71 MU for repair
T5419	13 EFTS	
T5421	13 EFTS	
T5426	13 EFTS	
T5490	10 FIS	
T5492	13 EFTS	
T5496	13 EFTS	
T5532	13 EFTS	
T5533	13 EFTS	
T5535	13 EFTS	
T5538	13 EFTS	
T5607	13 EFTS	
T5611	13 EFTS	
T5616	10 FIS	
T5698	10 FIS	Crashed 9-6-43, repaired
T5700	10 FIS	
T5882	13 EFTS	Crashed 2-12-40, repaired
T5896	10 FIS	Struck Off Charge 14-7-44
T5965	10 FIS	Crashed after control lost near Watlington, Oxfordshire 1-6-43
T5966	10 FIS	Struck Off Charge 14-1-44
T6169	10 FIS	
T6172	10 FIS	Struck Off Charge 14-7-44
T6175	10 FIS	
T6178	10 FIS	
T6198	10 FIS	
T6265	10 FIS	
T6269	10 FIS	
T6274	10 FIS	
T6318	10 FIS	

T6367	10 FIS	Damaged 27-9-44 and Struck Off Charge 4-10-44
T6570	10 FIS	
T6822	10 FIS	
T6905	10 FIS	Struck Off Charge 14-7-44
T6957	10 FIS	
T6986	10 FIS	Hit a tree on overshoot in a practice forced-landing Waltham St.Lawrence Emergency Landing Ground 16-10-43, pilot/instructor unhurt
T7016	13 EFTS	
T7020	10 FIS	
T7091	13 EFTS	
T7092	13 EFTS	
T7093	13 EFTS	
T7094	13 EFTS	
T7100	13 EFTS	
T7102	13 EFTS	
T7103	13 EFTS	
T7104	13 EFTS	
T7107	13 EFTS	
T7117	10 FIS	Hit a hedge on take-off from a forced-landing Warfield, Berkshire 13-11-44
T7121	10 FIS	
T7145	10 FIS	
T7162	13 EFTS	
T7176	8 EFTS	
T7212	13 EFTS	
T7235	13 EFTS	
T7261	8 EFTS	
T7305	8 EFTS	
T7307	8 EFTS, 10 FIS	
T7338	8 EFTS	
T7360	8 EFTS	
T7404	10 FIS	
T7445	10 FIS	
T7747	10 FIS	
T7784	10 FIS	Crashed 13-3-44, repaired
T7803	10 FIS	
T7840	10 FIS	
T7861	10 FIS	
T7994	10 FIS	
DE149	10 FIS	
DE152	10 FIS	
DE221	10 FIS	
DE364	10 FIS	
DE523	10 FIS	
DE567	10 FIS	
DE678	10 FIS	
DE718	10 FIS	
DE719	10 FIS	
DE773	10 FIS	
DE856	10 FIS	
DE873	10 FIS	
DE904	10 FIS	
DE936	10 FIS	Abandoned after controls jammed over Shiplake, Oxfordshire 22-8-43
DE943	10 FIS	Crashed 3-2-43, repaired
EM931	10 FIS	

NL764	10 FIS	
NL775	10 FIS	
NL776	10 FIS	
NL777	10 FIS	
NL778	10 FIS	
NL779	10 FIS	
NL780	10 FIS	
NL781	10 FIS	
NL782	10 FIS	
NL783	10 FIS	Hit the ground doing low aerobatics 3 miles North-West of Henley 21-2-44 (possibly crashed on farmland at Bix Manor, instructor and pupil killed)
NL784	10 FIS	
NM133	10 FIS	

Tiger Moth G-ADIA used by 13 EFTS as BB747 seen at Shenington airfield, Edgehill, Oxfordshire in August 2008 in the maroon and silver colours of the de Havilland School of Flying. (DJP)

The following Tiger Moths were impressed into RAF service from the de Havilland School of Flying at White Waltham

BB741	13 EFTS	ex G-ACDF	
BB742	13 EFTS	ex G-ACDI	
BB743	13 EFTS	ex G-ADHR	
BB744	13 EFTS	ex G-ADHS	
BB745	13 EFTS	ex G-ADHY	
BB746	13 EFTS	ex G-ADHZ	
BB747	13 EFTS	ex G-ADIA	
BB748	13 EFTS	ex G-ADIB	
BB749	13 EFTS	ex G-ADKG	
BB750	13 EFTS	ex G-ADLV	
BB751	13 EFTS	ex G-ADLW	
BB752	13 EFTS	ex G-ADLZ	
BB753	13 EFTS	ex G-ADMA	
BB754	13 EFTS	ex G-ADSH	Stalled on take-off and crashed 21-12-40 near Henley (possibly flown by LAC E. J. McGrath, killed, who is listed in the ORB for 13 EFTS has having an accident on this day)
BB755	13 EFTS	ex G-ADXE	
BB756	13 EFTS	ex G-ADXI	
BB757	13 EFTS	ex G-AELP	
BB758	13 EFTS	ex G-AEMF	
BB759	13 EFTS	ex G-AFGZ	
BB760	13 EFTS	ex G-AFJK	

One impressed Tiger Moth used by 8 EFTS

X5108	ex G-AFSJ of Newcastle-Upon-Tyne Aero Club

Miles Magister I

L5989	8 EFTS	
L5995	8 EFTS	
L5997	8 EFTS	
L6898	10 FIS	
L6915	8 EFTS	Crashed whilst low flying near Dene Camp, Camberley, Surrey 22-6-41 Sgt M Traisnel badly injured
L6918	8 EFTS	
L8065	8 EFTS, 10 FIS	
L8074	10 FIS	
L8128	8 EFTS, 10 FIS	
L8135	8 EFTS, 10 FIS	
L8145	8 EFTS, 10 FIS	
L8211	10 FIS	
L8219	8 EFTS	
L8257	8 EFTS, 10 FIS	Struck a tree during a forced-landing Waltham St.Lawrence ELG 16-3-43
L8283	8 EFTS	
L8353	8 EFTS, 10 FIS	P/O J.H. Ryan (Pilot) and LAC. A. Mortimer (Pupil) made a heavy wheel landing at Henley RLG aircraft slightly damaged 5-5-1942 (8 EFTS)
L8358	8 EFTS, 10 FIS	
N3800	8 EFTS, 10 FIS	
N3821	8 EFTS	
N3891	8 EFTS	
N3894	10 FIS	
N3942	8 EFTS	Crashed doing low aerobatics Warren Row near Maidenhead, Berkshire (possibly at Bottle Lane, Littlewick Green, Berkshire) 20-11-41 P/O J. N. Sellers was killed and Cpl J Wood badly injured
N3954	8 EFTS, 10 FIS	
N3955	8 EFTS, 10 FIS	
N3962	10 FIS	
N3969	8 EFTS	
N3983	8 EFTS, 10 FIS	
P2404	8 EFTS, 10 FIS	Aircraft collided with a paint sprayer at Henley 8-8-42 slightly damaged F/Lt R.C. Wright with LAC Watson (pupil) were uninjured
P2428	8 EFTS, 10 FIS	
P2454	8 EFTS	Hit trees on approach to Waltham St.Lawrence ELG 1-10-41 LAC F. Birchwood, killed
P2455	8 EFTS, 10 FIS	
P2462	8 EFTS, 10 FIS	
P6367	10 FIS	
P6369	8 EFTS, 10 FIS	
P6374	8 EFTS	
P6376	8 EFTS, 10 FIS	
P6406	8 EFTS, 10 FIS	
P6420	8 EFTS	
P6413	8 EFTS	
P6423	8 EFTS, 10 FIS	
P6438	8 EFTS, 10 FIS	
P6441	8 EFTS, 10 FIS	
P6445	8 EFTS	
P6448	8 EFTS	
R1842	8 EFTS, 10 FIS	
R1893	8 EFTS, 10 FIS	
R1895	8 EFTS	
R1900	8 EFTS, 10 FIS	Stalled at low altitude and crashed Ipsden, Oxfordshire 17-2-43

R1906	8 EFTS, 10 FIS	Spun into the ground near Woodley, Berkshire 14-11-44
R1907	8 EFTS	
R1908	8 EFTS	
R1909	8 EFTS	Dived into the ground at Chobham, Surrey 24-7-41
R1913	8 EFTS, 10 FIS	
R1983	8 EFTS	
T9684	10 FIS	
T9685	10 FIS	
T9686	8 EFTS, 10 FIS	
T9689	8 EFTS, 10 FIS	
T9690	8 EFTS, 10 FIS	
T9691	8 EFTS, 10 FIS	whilst carrying out a normal landing at Henley Relief Landing Ground, an accident occurred due to the right oleo leg of the undercarriage collapsing. Occupants uninjured. Plane slightly damaged 17-4-1942 F/Lt W.H.L. Dudley, A.F.C. (Pilot) LAC A. J. Caig (Pupil) (8 EFTS)
T9834	8 EFTS, 10 FIS	
T9893	8 EFTS, 10 FIS	
T9955	8 EFTS, 10 FIS	Made a heavy landing at Henley 23-5-42 aircraft slightly damaged Sgt. R. G. Langridge (Pilot) and LAC J. Woolman (Pupil) (8 EFTS)
T9956	8 EFTS, 10 FIS	
T9957	8 EFTS	
V1042	8 EFTS, 10 FIS	Spun into a farmhouse on take-off at Woodley, Berkshire 7-5-43
V1067	10 FIS	
V1072	8 EFTS, 10 FIS	Crashed whilst doing aerobatics over Henley-on-Thames 14-3-43
V1086	8 EFTS, 10 FIS	
V1087	8 EFTS, 10 FIS	

The following Magisters were impressed into RAF service from civil use

BB661	8 EFTS, 10 FIS	ex G-AFBS
BB662	8 EFTS, 10 FIS	ex G-AFDB Made a heavy landing at Henley 16-4-42 aircraft slightly damaged Pupil LAC I. D. Komaisavai uninjured (8 EFTS)
BB663	8 EFTS	ex G-AFTR
BB664	8 EFTS	ex G-AFTS Hit a high-tension cable and crashed Farley Hill, Berkshire 15-8-41 F/O R. M. Dryden and LAC F. C. Collins injured
BB665	8 EFTS	ex G-AFWY
BB666	8 EFTS, 10 FIS	ex G-AFXA
BB667	8 EFTS, 10 FIS	ex G-AFXB

Miles Magister BB661 ex civil G-AFBS used by 8 EFTS and 10 FIS preserved at the Imperial War Museum, Duxford. (DJP)

Miles Master I.
(Museum of Berkshire Aviation)

Miles Master I all used by 10 Flying Instructors School

N7439	Struck Off Charge 21-2-44
N7494	Struck Off Charge 25-2-44
N7673	Struck Off Charge 15-2-44
N7703	Crashed during a forced landing near Twyford, Berkshire 19-7-43
N7756	Struck Off Charge 25-2-44
N7757	Struck Off Charge 25-2-44
N7816	Struck Off Charge 25-2-44
N8042	Struck Off Charge 21-2-44
N8052	Struck Off Charge 12-2-44
T8384	Struck Off Charge 25-2-44
T8402	Struck Off Charge 15-2-44
T8446	Struck Off Charge 1-11-45
T8497	Crashed during a forced landing near Hurst, Berkshire 4-4-43
T8693	Struck Off Charge 21-2-44

Miles Master II DM327
of 10 Flying Instructors School
outside a Blister Hangar at Henley
(C. H. Thomas Collection)

Miles Master II & III all used by 10 Flying Instructors School

W9063	Crashed on landing at Woodley 15-6-44
AZ776	
AZ798	
AZ815	
AZ833	
DL350	Struck off charge 19-6-45
DL411	
DL969	Struck off charge 19-6-45
DM120	Struck off charge 19-6-45
DM136	Tail wheel collapsed during a heavy landing at Woodley 25-9-44
DM236	Sold as scrap 11-1-51
DM327	Sold as scrap 10-12-48
DM449	

SPITFIRES FROM GARAGES

During late 1940 Supermarine Aviation (Vickers) Ltd were looking for factories and airfields away from it's main factory in Southampton after bombing had seriously affected production of it's Spitfires at it's Itchen and Woolston works. Lord Beaverbrook, Minister of Aircraft Production met with Supermarine executives, and they decided on a dispersal scheme consisting of four separate production areas. One of the areas chosen was Reading, with the airfield at Henley which was to be used for the final assembly and test flying of the photo-reconnaissance version of the Spitfire the PR.IV. Other Spitfires were eventually assembled here including Mk.V fighter variants and the very first PR.XI's also used for photo-reconnaissance. Tools and jigs were sent to areas involved in production.

Various sites in Reading employing some 1,600 civilian workers under the management of Mr. Ken Scales, with Mr. Len G. Gooch as the Overall Works Manager, were to be used for sub-assembly of fuselages, wings and engines etc. the following factories and garages were involved:- Vincents Garage situated in Station Square, Reading made the fuselage and installed engines and also instrument panels and other detailing. Great Western Motors in Vastern Road, Reading assembled the wings and tailplane. Fuel tanks and other smaller parts including wing fairings and propeller spinners were made by Markhams, a coach-builders in Caversham Road and also by D. J. Hawkins Ltd in Erleigh Road, whose foreman panel-beater C. F. Taylor was in charge. The canteen was situated at the Central Garage in Reading. Anna Valley Motors in Salisbury were the sole producers of the wing-leading fuel tanks. The completed fuselages were taken to the Star Road works in nearby Caversham, here at this purpose built factory they were fitted out with the wiring, hydraulic lines, fuel and oil plumbing, tanks and other detailing, the engines were also installed here. The aircraft would then be loaded onto a Commer "Queen Mary" articulated low-loader and taken to Henley for final assembly by a team of around 30 people before being test flown and later delivered to a Maintenance Unit for fitting of operational equipment. Three Robins hangars as well as workshops, an air-raid shelter, petrol installation, stores and toilets were installed by the Air-Ministry in 1941 on the southern corner of the airfield for the assembly to take place. Spitfire assembly at Henley continued until the end of 1942, assembly and test flying of later photo-reconnaissance Spitfire PR.XI then continued in the Salisbury area at Chattis Hill and High Post airfields and also at Aldermaston from July 1943 until 1945. The reason for moving production away from Henley was because the later marks of more powerful photo-reconnaissance Spitfires needed a longer runway for take-off's and the runway length at Henley was considered to be to short. The hangars used for Spitfire production were placed on loan to the RAF in December 1944 and used by 529 (Rota) Squadron.

Other production units across the south of England who were also part of the Southern Regional Dispersal Scheme and also employed in assembly, included sites at Chandlers Ford, Chattis Hill, Hungerford, Hursley, Newbury, Trowbridge, Southampton, Westbury, Winchester and Wonston. Eventually there were 65 units spread over the Southern part of England, 46 of which were involved with production, with the remainder as support units. Other airfields used for the various dispersal sites were Chattis Hill, Chilbolton, High Post, Keevil and Worthy Down.

The underground factory situated at Warren Row near the airfield and run by Sir George Godfrey and Partners, was also involved in the manufacture of aircraft components such as vacuum-operated controls for aircraft of the Miles factory at Woodley, superchargers and various other parts were also produced here and these may well have been connected with Spitfire production at the airfield. Another site in Henley involved in aircraft manufacture again for the Miles factory was Talbot's Garage, here various departments were responsible for metal work.

Building a Spitfire

The Spitfire aircraft is of a monocoque construction built in three sections, the engine mounting, main fuselage section including cockpit area and finally the tail section. The fuselage consisting of frames which are assembled in a jig onto which a metal skin is then riveted. It is then removed from the jig ready to be placed in a another jig for the various holes for the wing sections to be drilled. The wing of a Spitfire is very complicated to build owing to it's unique elliptical shape, the leading edge being particularly difficult owing to the shape which is a D shaped section which formed the front spar, the main wing unit, the wing itself is made of sections called ribs. The next task to be completed was the fitting of the pintle, this was the pivot for the undercarriage and was attached to the rear spar section. Some of the Spitfires assembled at Henley were Mark V fighter variants, the gun bay's for these models were built in a separate jig before being installed into the main wing section. The radiators and wheel wells were next to be fitted into the wing area and when these had been installed the wing could then be skinned with metal, along with fitting of wiring, cables for the ailerons and piping for the guns, flaps and the landing lamps followed by aileron shrouds and the undercarriage itself before finally finishing it off with the access doors. The fuselage would then be finished with all the internal parts required, then the engine could be attached to the engine mounts followed by the cockpit interior, canopy and windscreen. The control surfaces would be connected up and the control column fitted as well as the pilots seat. Next up it was the turn of the fuel tank to be fitted which was followed by the heating and control systems, air, oil, electric's and hydraulics before attaching the wings. Final tests such as undercarriage retraction could then be carried out before the final task of fitting the propeller after which the engine could be ground run for testing. After this had all been successfully carried out test flying could begin. There were believed to be ten to twelve test pilots employed by Vickers-Supermarine Southern Region who were based at High Post, under the leadership of Jeffrey Quill, they also included George Pickering, Colin Jarred and John Wakefield, others came from the Fleet Air Arm, RAF and some from overseas, and they would fly to the individual airfields by light aircraft. A standard test lasted about 40 minutes and included checks for performance and handling, and some adjustments might have been necessary after the flight. When test flying had been completed the aircraft would then be signed off and ready to be collected by the men and women pilots of the Air Transport Auxiliary (ATA) a civilian organisation who would be flown in usually by an Avro Anson or Fairchild Argus taxi aircraft from White Waltham, Hamble or one of their other locations ready to ferry the Spitfire to a Maintenance Unit for fitting of the operational equipment.

The main components of a Spitfire before assembly.

Vickers-Armstrongs Employees
Working at Reading, Henley and Aldermaston

Many men and women were employed by Vickers-Armstrongs at their dispersal sites during the war, some were chosen because they lived close to these sites, however others had to be found local accommodation or be bused to the location. Mrs Florence Mitchell, the wife of the late Spitfire designer Reginald J. Mitchell, worked as a voluntary driver and would often travel once a week to the airfield at Henley with coupons for the civilian workers.

One employee was Gordon Painter who was born in April 1916 and lived in Henley-on-Thames. He started work as a motor mechanic, and was apprenticed for the sum of £10 which was paid out on completion of his training, working at Caversham Motors (1920) Ltd in Church Street, Caversham for 4 years starting in May 1933. He is likely to have answered an advert for tradesmen and started work for Vickers-Armstrongs Supermarine during May 1941. His work involved assembling and checking undercarriage oleo hydraulics and tyre pressures, and pintle assembly. The pintle being the part of the undercarriage which is attached to the main wing spar on which the undercarriage retracts. He worked on the majority of Spitfire PR.IV and V aircraft assembled at Henley before he relocated in December 1942 to Chattis Hill near Winchester working on many different Spitfire variants from VIII and IX to the early PR.XI, then moving onto Aldermaston in January 1944 when Spitfire production relocated there. Here he was involved in working on later marks of Spitfires such as the PR.XI, XIV and XVIII. It is likely that having been issued his own tools that he travelled to other airfields for work including Benson. (with thanks to David & Diana Painter)

Vickers-Armstrongs employee Gordon Painter

The Spitfire undercarriage pintle which is attached to the main wing spar.

Label inside the tool box indicating that it was issued to Vickers-Armstrongs workers.

Spitfire wheel Pintle spanner, used by Gordon Painter, The Pintle is the pivot on which the undercarriage retracts.

A Vickers-Armstrongs toolbox
issued to workers.

Vickers-Armstrongs workers pose in front of a
Spitfire XVIII at Aldermaston.
(Gordon Painter)

Vickers-Armstrongs workers at Vincents Garage in Reading.

A PR Spitfire back in Berkshire, PR.XI PL965 seen here at White Waltham in August 2007, a short distance from Reading where many of the PR Spitfires were constructed and very close to Henley where they were assembled and test flown. This particular example was built in Reading and assembled and test flown at Aldermaston which had taken over from Henley, and it first flew in 1944. This aircraft was worked on by Gordon Painter during his time at Aldermaston. (DJP)

The following photographs showing assembly of Spitfires and Spitfire components at Vincents Garage, and Great Western Motors in Reading, and Star Road in Caversham were loaned to the Museum of Berkshire Aviation at Woodley by former ATA pilot Lettice Curtis.

Vincents Garage, Station Square, Reading

The exterior of Vincents Garage, in Station Square, Reading. note the showroom windows have been boarded up.

The interior of Vincents Garage, here they are making sub-assembly parts ready for fitting to a fuselage.

Spitfires under construction at Vincents Garage, both fighter and PR Spitfires can be seen.
Work is being carried out on the cowling and in the fuel tank area of a PR.IV version on the left.

Great Western Motors, Vastern Road, Reading

Wings under construction in a jig at Vastern Road.

The Star Road Factory, Caversham

Vickers-Armstrongs Spitfire Assembly at Henley

Spitfire PR.IV's under final assembly in the Robins Hangar, Airfield layout location 101
(both supplied by Eloise Morton, River & Rowing Museum, Henley)

A tie-down ring, located outside the assembly hangar, an aircraft would be tied
down with a strap and ropes whilst undergoing engine runs. (Nigel Dawe)

SPITFIRE PR.IV

The PR IV based on the fuselage of the Mk.V with a Merlin 45 or 46 engine, had the longest range of any of the early PR Spitfires. It could carry 66 gallons of fuel in each wing, giving it a range of 2000 miles, a tank fitted in the port wing of 18 gallons provided the necessary oil to go with the fuel. It entered service in October 1940, and was produced in much larger numbers than any other early PR Spitfire. The Spitfire PR.IV was known as the "bowser" because of the amount of fuel it could carry. The PR.IV was the first PR Spitfire to feature a heated cockpit and drinking water. The paint finish of these Spitfires was a tint of blue known as 'PR blue'.

Type 353 Spitfire PR.IV
Engine: One 1,440hp Rolls-Royce Merlin 45 or 46 liquid-cooled V12 piston engine
One Rotol RX5/10 or de Havilland 5/39B 3-blade propeller with a diameter of 10 feet 9 inches

Dimensions
Span: 36 feet 10 inches (11.23m)
Length: 29 feet 11 inches (9.12m)
Height: 8 feet 2¼ inches (2.50m)

Weights
Empty: 4,953 lb (2,247kg)
Loaded: 7,155lb (3,246kg) when carrying 'X' camera installation

Performance:
Maximum speed: 372 mph (323 Knots, 599 km/h)
Service ceiling: 38,000 feet (11,582m)
some aircraft were modified by 103 Maintenance Unit at Aboukir, Egypt the tropical intake filter being modified to a much smaller unit which was more efficient.
No armament was carried

The PR IV could carry a wide variety of camera installations, each given a letter code as follows:
W: Two F.8 with 20in focal length, this installation is an alternative to the X type
X: One F.24 with 14in focal length, this installation is an alternative to the W type
Y: One F.52 with 36in focal length, this camera is placed in a fixed vertical position

Cameras were heated to stop them freezing up at altitude either by hot air from the engine or electrically.

The following pages are a production list of the Spitfires known to have been assembled and flown from Henley, although there are a few that are not certain, and these are marked with a *. The serial number of the aircraft comes first and to the right of that is the build number which was allocated by Vickers-Supermarine at Southampton. The history is then shown from first flight date, where known and then the subsequent service history of the aircraft. In some cases the flying hours are known and these are also included. Accidents and incidents were often allocated a type of Category followed by a letter, the following is a list explaining these.

Category.A   Minor damage, can be repaired by a unit
Category.AC   Minor damage, not repairable by a unit
Category.B   Not repairable on site
Category.C   To be used for ground instruction
Category.E   Aircraft considered a write-off

Vickers-Armstrongs (Supermarine) Spitfires assembled & test flown at Henley-on-Thames
Individual aircraft histories

5 Spitfire Mk.1 converted to PR.V and PR.VI
Contract No. B19713/39 Third order

X4502   1632
4-2-1941   Contract loan, to Heston Aircraft Ltd, Middlesex
3-5-1941   converted to PR.V Type C
29-6-1941   1 Photographic Reconnaissance Unit, Benson, Oxfordshire
4-9-1941   Category.B accident on operations to Heston Aircraft Ltd
13-9-1941   1 Photographic Reconnaissance Unit, Benson
               Heston Aircraft Ltd converted to PR.VI Type F
18-11-1941   1 Photographic Reconnaissance Unit, Benson
22-4-1942   140 Army Co-operation School, Bircham Newton, Norfolk
2-6-1942   Missing from a PR mission to Cherbourg, France, presumed shot down. P/O F. J. Blackwood (k)
Total Flying Hours 177.45

X4503   1644
               First Flight
8-5-1941   Director General of Research & Development, Farnborough, Hampshire
30-9-1941   Heston Aircraft Ltd converted to PR.V Type C
3-10-1941   1 Photographic Reconnaissance Unit, Benson
11-41   1401 Meteorological Flight, Bircham Newton
15-3-1942   Failed to return from a Meteorological Flight
               Shot down and crashed 1 mile west of Lopikerkapel, Holland. W/C Jock. W. S. Forbes (k)

X4504   1655
               First Flight
11-5-1941   Director General of Research & Development, Farnborough
17-5-1941   Heston Aircraft Ltd converted to PR.V Type C
8-7-1941   1 Photographic Reconnaissance Unit, Benson
11-7-1941   Engine failed and aircraft force-landed and hit a telegraph pole, Nordelph, Norfolk.
7-1941   43 Group Disposal Account
31-7-1941   Struck off charge

X4505   1687
16-3-1941   Contract loan, to Heston Aircraft Ltd
20-5-1941   converted to PR.V Type C
12-9-1941   1 Photographic Reconnaissance Unit, Benson
26-1-1942   Flying Accident Category.AC
               Heston Aircraft Ltd converted to PR.VI Type F
26-7-1942   8 Operational Training Unit, Fraserburgh, Aberdeenshire
31-5-1943   Pilot blacked-out due to lack of oxygen, aircraft dived into the ground Cotes Farm
Total Flying Hours 200.10

X4538   1693
16-3-1941   Contract loan, to Heston Aircraft Ltd converted to PR.V Type C
22-5-1941   Director General of Research & Development, Farnborough for trials
19-8-1941   1 Photographic Reconnaissance Unit, Benson
25-12-1941   Crashed on landing Benson. Category.B
15-1-1942   Struck off charge

6 Aircraft built and flown as Mk.V converted to PR.IV Type C and D
Contract No. B19713/39 First order

R7029	1688
21-5-1941	First Flight
22-5-1941	Heston Aircraft Ltd for conversion to PRIV Type C
14-7-1941	1 Photographic Reconnaissance Unit, Benson
27-7-1941	Flying accident Category.AC to Heston Aircraft Ltd for repair
9-1941	1 Photographic Reconnaissance Unit, Benson
27-4-1942	Dived into ground Cookley Green, near Benson, Oxfordshire. Sgt L. Branton (k)
28-4-1942	Struck off charge

R7030	1694
22-5-1941	First Flight
24-5-1941	Royal Aircraft Establishment, Farnborough
30-5-1941	Heston Aircraft Ltd for conversion to PRIV Type D
30-10-1941	1 Photographic Reconnaissance Unit, Benson
26-1-1942	Flying accident Category.AC repaired on site
20-6-1942	8 Operational Training Unit, Fraserburgh
14-1-1943	Heston Aircraft Ltd
6-3-1943	6 Maintenance Unit, Brize Norton, Oxfordshire
13-3-1943	Heston Aircraft Ltd
3-7-1944	Air Service Training, Exeter, Devon

R7031	1714
5-1941	First Flight
30-5-1941	Heston Aircraft Ltd for conversion to PRIII Type C
24-7-1941	1 Photographic Reconnaissance Unit, Benson
9-9-1941	General Aircraft Ltd, Feltham, Middlesex
10-9-1941	Heston Aircraft Ltd for conversion PRIV Type D
16-4-1942	1 Satellite Landing Ground (39 MU), Slade Farm near Wootton, Oxfordshire
1-8-1942	8 Operational Training Unit, Fraserburgh
21-8-1942	Photographic Reconnaissance Unit, Fraserburgh
30-8-1942	Heston Aircraft Ltd
4-5-1943	Flying accident Category.E
10-1-1944	Scottish Aviation Ltd, Prestwick, Ayreshire
31-3-1945	1 Satellite Landing Ground (39 MU), Slade Farm near Wootton, Oxfordshire for storage
4-4-1945	Struck off charge

R7032	1715
5-1941	First Flight
31-5-1941	Royal Aircraft Establishment, as a PRIII Type C
1-8-1941	1 Photographic Reconnaissance Unit, Benson
27-8-1942	Flying accident Category.B
31-8-1942	Heston Aircraft Ltd for conversion to PRIV Type D
3-9-1942	Benson
18-1-1943	8 Operational Training Unit, Fraserburgh
15-3-1943	Flying accident Category.AC repaired on site
9-2-1944	6 Maintenance Unit, Brize Norton converted to PRVI Type F
6-3-1945	Struck off charge

R7033   1738
           First Flight
8-6-1941   Heston Aircraft Ltd for conversion to PRIII Type C
7-8-1941   1 Photographic Reconnaissance Unit, Benson
5-10-1941   Suffered loss of control in storm at high altitude and crashed near Bishops Stortford, Herts
1-1942   Remains to Royal Aircraft Establishment, Farnborough

R7034   1755
           First Flight
7-6-1941   Royal Aircraft Establishment, Farnborough
           converted to PRIII Type C later to PRV then to Special PRV
2-4-1942   Flying Accident Category.B repaired on site
4-8-1942   Used on high altitude trials
19-11-1942 Empire Test Pilots School, Boscombe Down,Wiltshire for air homing trials
4-1943   Engine changed to Sunbeam Talbot
4-1943   Royal Aircraft Establishment, Farnborough trials for cooling and drag reduction modifications
6-1943   Peterborough, chemistry application trials
12-6-43   To Gibraltar for temperature rating tests, flew around the Middle East
           from Gibraltar-Maison Blanche, Tripoli-Cairo, Tripoli-Malta, Algiers-Gibraltar, had jettison
           overload tanks, main purpose of the test was validity of tropical filters and various cooling.
15-7-1943 Returned to Farnborough
8-1943   Flexi-tank trials, tanks later fitted to Bristol Blenheims and de Havilland Mosquitos
19-1-1944 used in reconnaissance trials with a Spitfire IX
6-44   trials for TR1996 radio
20-11-1946 ACR trials with Blackburn Firebrand EK670
           VHF and SBA trials
           to RAF film unit at Hucknall for photo sessions with Avro Lancaster FM201
1-4-1950   Struck off charge
           Used as a station hack at Farnborough until 1954, replaced by Seafire SX342

12 Aircraft built and flown as Mk.V PR.C converted to PR.IV type C and D

R7035   1838
7-7-1941   Heston Aircraft Ltd for conversion to PRIV Type D
7-1941   First Flight as a PRIV
23-12-1941 1 Photographic Reconnaissance Unit, Benson
19-2-1942 1 Photographic Reconnaissance Unit, Leuchars, Fife
18-3-1942 Failed to return from a PR mission to Stavanger, Norway

R7036   1856
7-7-1941   Heston Aircraft Ltd for conversion to PRIV Type C
           First Flight as a PRIV
7-8-1941   1 Photographic Reconnaissance Unit, Benson
12-4-1942 Failed to return from a PR mission to Bremerhaven, Germany

R7037   1901
7-7-1941   Heston Aircraft Ltd for conversion to PRIV Type D
16-7-1941 First Flight as a PRIV
2-8-1941   1 Photographic Reconnaissance Unit, Benson
15-10-1941 Heston Aircraft Ltd for modifications
16-12-1941 1 Photographic Reconnaissance Unit, Benson
3-6-1942   Shot down and crashed Valognes whilst on a PR mission to Cherbourg-Le Havre, France
           Joseph Campbell McPherson (k)

R7038   1922
7-7-1941   Heston Aircraft Ltd for conversion to PRIV Type D
19-7-1941   First Flight as a PRIV
8-1941   1 Photographic Reconnaissance Unit, Benson
19-12-1941 Heston Aircraft Ltd converted to PRVI Type F
             1 Photographic Reconnaissance Unit, Benson
2-1-1942   Flying accident Category.B repaired on site
16-9-1942   Failed to return form a PR mission to Bremen and Wilhelmshaven, Germany.
             P/O Ian Gurth Barraclough (PoW)

R7039   1943
7-7-1941   Heston Aircraft Ltd for conversion to PRIV Type D
2-8-1941   First Flight as a PRIV
8-1941   Royal Aircraft Establishment, for trials
18-8-1941   1 Photographic Reconnaissance Unit, Benson
10-9-1941   Failed to return from a PR mission over the French/Spanish frontier

R7040   1944
7-7-1941   Heston Aircraft Ltd for conversion to PRIV Type D
2-8-1941   First Flight as a PRIV
12-8-1941   1 Photographic Reconnaissance Unit, Benson
2-12-1941   Failed to return from a PR mission to Brest, France. Sgt Leonard Briggs (k)

R7041   1945
6-8-1941   First Flight as a PRIV by test pilot George Pickering
16-8-1941   to Chattis Hill
17-8-1941   1 Photographic Reconnaissance Unit, Benson
30-3-1942   Flying accident Category.B
6-4-1942   Heston Aircraft Ltd for repairs
19-10-1942 541 Squadron, Benson
12-1-1943   Failed to return from a PR mission to Kristiansand, Norway

R7042   1946
8-8-1941   First Flight as a PRIV by test pilot George Pickering
16-8-1941   Chattis Hill
19-8-1941   1 Photographic Reconnaissance Unit, Benson
19-10-1942 541 Squadron, Benson
16-2-1943   Crashed at Whitfield, Brackley, Buckinghamshire on a cross-country flight to Whitby, Yorkshire
             Sgt J. P. Power (k)

R7043   1971
7-7-1941   Heston Aircraft Ltd for conversion to PRIV Type D
9-8-1941   First Flight as a PRIV
21-8-1941   1 Photographic Reconnaissance Unit, Benson
30-9-1941   Failed to return from a PR mission to Kiel, Germany

R7044   1972
7-7-1941   Heston Aircraft Ltd for conversion to PRIV Type D
13-8-1941   First Flight as a PRIV
22-8-1941   1 Photographic Reconnaissance Unit, Benson
16-2-1942   1 Photographic Reconnaissance Unit, Wick
27-4-1942   Force landed in a field due to engine failure on Copinsay Island, Orkneys.
             flown by F/Lt William.Ronald Acott, Category.B to Heston Aircraft Ltd for repair
12-11-1942 541 Squadron, Benson
13-1-1943   Failed to return from a PR mission from Stadlandet to Karno, Norway
             W/O William J. Payne (missing)

R7055	1996
7-7-1941	Heston Aircraft Ltd for conversion to PRIV Type D
24-8-1941	First Flight as a PRIV
26-8-1941	Vickers-Armstrongs Ltd, Henley-on-Thames
28-8-1941	1 Photographic Reconnaissance Unit, Benson
15-4-1942	1 Photographic Reconnaissance Unit, Gibraltar
15-4-1942	Lost power on overshoot during landing Gibraltar and ditched into sea. Category.E
26-4-1942	Struck off charge

R7056	1997
7-7-1941	Heston Aircraft Ltd for conversion to PRIV Type D
24-8-1941	First Flight as a PRIV
26-8-1941	Vickers-Armstrongs Ltd, Henley-on-Thames
28-8-1941	1 Photographic Reconnaissance Unit, Benson
10-4-1942	Shot down on a PR mission to St. Malo, Morlaix, Lannion and St. Brieuc, France F/O John Butler Ayer (k)
12-4-1942	Struck off charge

Aircraft built and flown as PR.IV type D Contract No. B19713/39 Fourth order

AA781   1998
21-8-1941   First Flight
28-8-1941   1 Photographic Reconnaissance Unit, Benson
6-1-1942   Flying Accident Category.AC repaired on site
1-8-1942   Failed to return from a PR mission to Vegesack, Germany

AA782   1999
22-8-1941   First Flight
30-8-1941   1 Photographic Reconnaissance Unit, Benson (detachment to Wick)
12-11-1941 Engine cut on take-off and aircraft crash landed, Wick. Category.B
29-11-1941 Struck off charge

AA783   2000
24-8-1941   First Flight
30-8-1941   1 Photographic Reconnaissance Unit, Benson
8-11-1941   Heston Aircraft Ltd
6-2-1942   1 Photographic Reconnaissance Unit, Benson
13-3-1942   Shot down by FW190 on a PR mission to Wilhelmshaven, Germany. crashed Jelsum
              P/O MacDonald, safe

AA784   2005
26-8-1941   First Flight
30-8-1941   1 Photographic Reconnaissance Unit, Benson
26-1-1942   Heston Aircraft Ltd for Merlin 46 installation
11-6-1942   Category.B accident on operations
24-6-1942   1 Photographic Reconnaissance Unit, Benson
19-10-1942 542 Squadron, Benson
5-5-1943   8 Operational Training Unit, Dyce, Aberdeenshire
17-6-1943   Flying accident Category.AC
30-12-1944 Struck off charge

AA785   2018
27-8-1941   First Flight
30-9-1941   1 Photographic Reconnaissance Unit, Benson (fitted with a 'W' type camera installation)
7-10-1941   Force-landed at Nova Scotia Farm, West Caister, Norfolk returning from PR to Copenhagen.
              Sgt Mervyn A. Jones (OK)
13-10-1941 Heston Aircraft Ltd
12-4-1942   3 Satellite Landing Ground (8 MU), Middle Farm near Mixbury, Oxfordshire
2-10-1942   1 Photographic Reconnaissance Unit, Benson
19-10-1942 542 Squadron, Benson
15-9-1943   1 Overseas Aircraft Delivery Unit, Portreath, Cornwall
11-1943   681 Squadron, Dum Dum, Calcutta, India to Middle East
5-6-1945   Struck off charge

AA786   2031
29-8-1941   First Flight
6-9-1941   1 Photographic Reconnaissance Unit, Benson
2-1-1942   Heston Aircraft Ltd for modifications
11-1-1942   1 Photographic Reconnaissance Unit, Benson
12-2-1942   Flying accident Category.AC
5-2-1943   Benson
6-9-1943   1 Overseas Aircraft Delivery Unit, Portreath
7-10-1943   681 Squadron, Dum Dum, Calcutta, India
5-4-1945   Swung on take-off and tipped up on soft ground, Jodphur, India. Category.E
31-5-1945   Struck off charge

AA787   2044
4-9-1941   First Flight
6-9-1941   1 Photographic Reconnaissance Unit, Benson
23-2-1942   Failed to return from a PR mission to Katwijk, Holland. F/Lt E. J. Durston

AA788   2052
4-9-1941   First Flight by test pilot George Pickering
9-9-1941   1 Photographic Reconnaissance Unit, Benson
13-10-1941 Heston Aircraft Ltd
17-9-1942   Benson
27-9-1942   8 Operational Training Unit, Fraserburgh
6-6-1943   Flying accident Category.B to Heston Aircraft Ltd for repair
9-1943   8 Operational Training Unit, Dyce
20-7-1944   Engine lost power and aircraft belly-landed 1 mile West of Fordoun, Aberdeenshire. Category.B
14-8-1944   Re: Category.E

AA789   2053
5-9-1941   First Flight
9-9-1941   1 Photographic Reconnaissance Unit, Benson
12-12-1941 Heston Aircraft Ltd for modifications
26-1-1942   1 Photographic Reconnaissance Unit, Leuchars, Fife
2-1943   Benson
4-1943   1 Overseas Aircraft Delivery Unit, Portreath
5-1943   680 Squadron, Heliopolis, Egypt
30-11-1944 Struck off charge

AA790   2074
12-9-1941   First Flight by test pilot George Pickering
13-9-1941   1 Photographic Reconnaissance Unit, Benson (fitted with a X type camera installation)
6-6-1942   Flying Accident Category.B to Heston Aircraft Ltd
19-10-1942 541 Squadron, Benson
9-1-1943   540 Squadron, Leuchars
21-6-1943   8 Operational Training Unit, Dyce
8-9-1943   Vickers-Armstrongs Supermarine Ltd - external sump wing oil tank modification
11-1943   8 Operational Training Unit, Dyce
15-12-1944 Lost power and belly-landed in a field, Westburn Farm, Dunning near Auchterarder, Perth
1-1-1945   Struck off charge

AA791   2075
12-9-1941   First Flight
13-9-1941   1 Photographic Reconnaissance Unit, Benson (fitted with a X type camera installation)
22-4-1942   Flying Accident Category.AC
13-10-1942 Controller of Research & Development, Vickers-Armstrongs, Worthy Down, Hampshire
19-11-1942 Benson
14-12-1942 542 Squadron, Benson
6-6-1943   Collided with Spitfire BM350 and crashed near Nettlebed, Oxfordshire. Category.E

AA792   2077
13-9-1941   First Flight
13-9-1941   1 Photographic Reconnaissance Unit, Benson
7-12-1941   Ditched in the Gulf of St.Malo on a PR mission to Brest, France. F/Lt John Burke Hatchwell (k)

AA793   2091
15-9-1941   First Flight
18-9-1941   1 Photographic Reconnaissance Unit, Benson (fitted with a X type camera installation)
16-5-1942   Flying accident Category.C
19-10-1942 542 Squadron, Benson
18-12-1942 Flying accident Category.B
5-5-1943   1 Overseas Aircraft Delivery Unit, Portreath
31-5-1943   681 Squadron, Dum Dum, Calcutta (aircraft coded 'F')
28-10-1943 Lost on a sortie to Indaw, Burma. F/Sgt Hain

AA794   2094
16-9-1941   First Flight
18-9-1941   1 Photographic Reconnaissance Unit, Benson (fitted with a X type camera installation)
7-11-1941   Heston Aircraft Ltd for modifications
18-11-1941 1 Photographic Reconnaissance Unit, Benson
27-9-1942   8 Operational Training Unit, Fraserburgh
12-7-1943   Engine failed and aircraft made a wheels-up landing, Fraserburgh. Category.E

AA795   2113
19-9-1941   First Flight
25-9-1941   1 Photographic Reconnaissance Unit, Benson
10-12-1941 Heston Aircraft Ltd
            1 Photographic Reconnaissance Unit, Benson
24-4-1942   Failed to return from a PR mission to Amiens, France

AA796   2115
20-9-1941   First Flight by by test pilot George Pickering
25-9-1941   1 Photographic Reconnaissance Unit, Benson
12-12-1941 Heston Aircraft Ltd for modifications
12-1941   1 Photographic Reconnaissance Unit, Benson
30-12-1941 Failed to return from a PR mission to Brest, France. S/L T.D. Calnan (PoW)

AA797   2148
30-9-1941   First Flight
1-10-1941   1 Photographic Reconnaissance Unit, Benson
30-11-1941 Heston Aircraft Ltd for modifications
10-12-1941 1 Photographic Reconnaissance Unit, Benson
3-4-1942   Failed to return from a PR mission to Trondheim, Norway. F/Sgt Mervyn A. Jones (k)

AA798   2143
29-9-1941   First Flight
1-10-1941   1 Photographic Reconnaissance Unit, Benson
2-2-1942   General Aircraft Ltd, Feltham
6-2-1942   1 Photographic Reconnaissance Unit, St.Eval, Cornwall
12-4-1942   Crashed at Wickham, Berkshire on route for a PR mission to Rotterdam, Holland. Category.E

AA799   2144
29-9-1941   First Flight by test pilot George Pickering
2-10-1941   1 Photographic Reconnaissance Unit, Benson
11-2-1943   Heston Aircraft Ltd
20-5-1943   Benson
9-6-1943   1 Overseas Aircraft Delivery Unit, Portreath
16-6-1943   681 Squadron, Dum Dum, Calcutta (aircraft coded 'M')
26-9-1944   Undercarriage not locked down and aircraft belly-landed, Alipore, India
5-10-1944   Struck off charge

AA800   2145
29-9-1941   First Flight by test pilot George Pickering
1-10-1941   1 Photographic Reconnaissance Unit, Benson
              Heston Aircraft Ltd for modifications
8-12-1941   1 Photographic Reconnaissance Unit, Benson
30-7-1942   Failed to return from a PR mission to Bergen, Norway
31-7-1942   Struck off charge
Total Flying Hours 155.10

AA801   2146
29-9-1941   First Flight
7-10-1941   1 Photographic Reconnaissance Unit, Benson
29-10-1941 Aircraft suffered structural failure in flight and crashed near Watchfield, Berkshire
1-1942   Royal Aircraft Establishment Accident Investigation Unit
5-11-1942   Struck off charge

AA802   2147
30-9-1941   First Flight
5-10-1941   1 Photographic Reconnaissance Unit, Benson
7-9-1942   Failed to return from a PR mission to Bremen, Germany. F/Lt William John Scafe (k)
8-9-1942   Struck off charge
Total Flying Hours 25.55

AA803   2160
2-10-1941   First Flight
5-10-1941   1 Photographic Reconnaissance Unit, Benson (fitted with a W type camera installation)
15-1-1942   Flying accident Category.B
19-10-1942 543 Squadron, Benson, Mount Farm & St.Eval
11-3-1943   1 Overseas Aircraft Delivery Unit, Portreath
14-3-1943   Ferry flight to North Africa
3-1943   682 Squadron, Maison Blanche, Algiers, Algeria
5-5-1943   Aircraft abandoned 14 miles North of Algiers on returning from Marseille, France

AA804   2166
6-10-1941   First Flight
7-10-1941   1 Photographic Reconnaissance Unit, Benson
30-11-1941 Heston Aircraft Ltd for modifications
7-12-1941   1 Photographic Reconnaissance Unit, Benson
28-12-1941 Failed to return from a PR mission to Dusseldorf, Germany.
              Presumed crashed, Burgen Op Zoom, Holland F/Lt Charles P. Hall (PoW)

AA805   2167
6-10-1941   First Flight
7-10-1941   1 Photographic Reconnaissance Unit, Benson
13-2-1942   On returning from a PR mission, aircraft overshot on landing in cross-wind, Benson
              P/O L. L. Whitaker (injured)
22-2-1942   Struck off charge

AA806   2195
14-10-1941 First Flight
19-10-1941 1 Photographic Reconnaissance Unit, Benson
19-10-1942 543 Squadron, Benson, Mount Farm, Oxfordshire & St.Eval
28-10-1942 Failed to return from a PR mission to Cherbourg, France Sgt Luepke (missing)
Total Flying Hours 238

AA807   2176
9-10-1941 First Flight
13-10-1941 1 Photographic Reconnaissance Unit, Benson (fitted with a W type camera installation)
19-2-1942 Flying accident Category.E on operations
19-10-1942 541 Squadron, Benson
16-4-1943 Flying accident Category.B on operations
21-6-1943 543 Squadron, Benson, Mount Farm & St.Eval
19-10-1943 Heston Aircraft Ltd for Merlin 46 Installation
19-3-1944 4 Squadron, Sawbridgeworth, Hertfordshire
12-3-1945 Struck off charge

AA808   2185
11-10-1941 First Flight by test pilot George Pickering
13-10-1941 1 Photographic Reconnaissance Unit, Benson (fitted with a W type camera installation)
18-2-1942 Heston Aircraft Ltd for modifications
30-9-1942 541 Squadron, Benson
15-2-1943 Flying accident Category.AC
4-3-1943 Flying accident Category.B on operations
7-7-1943 543 Squadron, Benson, Mount Farm & St.Eval
10-8-1943 Air Service Training Ltd, Hamble, Hampshire

AA809   2207
17-10-1941 First Flight
19-10-1941 1 Photographic Reconnaissance Unit, Benson
19-10-1942 543 Squadron, Benson, Mount Farm & St.Eval
13-2-1943 Failed to return from a PR mission to Lorient, France. F/O G. B. D. Greenwood (k)

AA810   2203
17-10-1941 First Flight
19-10-1941 1 Photographic Reconnaissance Unit, Benson (detachment to Wick)
5-3-1942 took off from Wick a/f at 08.07 hrs, Shot down on a PR mission to Trondheim, Norway
    and crashed 95km WSW of Trondheim. F/Lt Alistair D. M. Gunn (PoW)

AA811   2208
19-10-1941 First Flight
20-10-1941 1 Photographic Reconnaissance Unit, Benson (fitted with a W camera)
19-10-1942 543 Squadron, Benson, Mount Farm & St.Eval
3-7-1943 On returning from a PR mission to Lannion, France the engine cut-out and the aircraft was
    abandoned 60 miles South of the Lizard, Cornwall. F/O Rothwell

AA812   2213
22-10-1941 First Flight
24-10-1941 1 Photographic Reconnaissance Unit, Benson
24-1-1942 Bounced on landing and hit a snow bank, Topcliffe, Yorkshire
27-1-1942 Struck off charge

AA813   2219
24-10-1941 First Flight by test pilot George Pickering
28-10-1941 1 Photographic Reconnaissance Unit, Benson
25-1-1942 Engine cut out and aircraft force-landed on Chesil Bank, Dorset. F/O M.C.B. Anderson

AA814   2221
25-10-1941 First Flight
26-10-1941 1 Photographic Reconnaissance Unit, Benson
17-8-1942 Failed to return from a PR mission to Wilhelmshaven, Kiel and Emden, Germany
    aircraft shot down by FW.190's and crashed Süderoog Sand. P/O Andre Cantillion (k)

AA815   2234
28-10-1941 First Flight as a PR.IV(T)
30-10-1941 1 Photographic Reconnaissance Unit, Benson
11-4-1942 Flying accident Category.AC to Heston Aircraft Ltd for repair
29-4-1943 1 Overseas Aircraft Delivery Unit, Portreath
1-5-1943   680 Squadron, Heliopolis, Egypt
            74 Operational Training Unit, Petah Tiqva, Palestine
8-3-1945   Swung on landing and undercarriage collapsed on soft ground, Petah Tiqva
31-5-1945 Struck off charge

AB118   2244
30-10-1941 First Flight
3-11-1941 1 Photographic Reconnaissance Unit, Benson
19-10-1942 542 Squadron, Benson
27-10-1942 Flying accident Category.AC
4-2-1943   140 Squadron, Benson/St.Eval
11-12-1943 Heston Aircraft Ltd Merlin 46 Installation
22-4-1945 Struck off charge

AB119   2259
31-10-1941 First Flight
6-11-1941 1 Photographic Reconnaissance Unit, Benson
11-1-1942 Flying accident Category.AC Repaired on site
18-4-1942 Failed to return from a PR mission to St.Malo, France
Total Flying Hours 76.45

AB120   2270
5-11-1941 First Flight
6-11-1941 1 Photographic Reconnaissance Unit, Benson
11-8-1942 Failed to return from a PR mission to Kiel, Germany

AB121   2271
7-11-1941 First Flight
11-11-1941 5 Maintenance Unit, Kemble, Gloucestershire
11-12-1941 Northolt Dispersal
3-1-1942   Vickers-Armstrongs Ltd, Henley-on-Thames
27-6-1942 1 Photographic Reconnaissance Unit, Benson
19-10-1942 542 Squadron, Benson
19-10-1942 Shot down over the Schneider Works at Le Creusot, France
            S/L Anthony Eustace Hill (C/O of 543 Sqn) died in hospital in Dijon
Total Flying Hours 49.55

AB122   2281
8-11-1941 First Flight
11-11-1941 5 Maintenance Unit, Kemble
11-12-1941 Northolt Dispersal
9-3-1942   Vickers-Armstrongs Ltd, Henley-on-Thames
22-6-1942 140 Squadron, Benson/St.Eval
19-7-1942 Flying accident Category.A on operation, P/O L. G. Smith
            Heston Aircraft Ltd Merlin 46 Installation
7-11-1942 8 Operational Training Unit, Fraserburgh
15-9-1943 Flying accident Category.AC
6-11-1943 Vickers-Armstrongs Supermarine Ltd - external sump wing oil tank modification
1-1944   8 Operational Training Unit, Dyce
16-3-1945 Struck off charge

AB123   2282
8-11-1941 First Flight
12-11-1941 5 Maintenance Unit, Kemble
3-1-1942   Vickers-Armstrongs Ltd, Henley-on-Thames
16-4-1942 1 Photographic Reconnaissance Unit, Benson
19-10-1942 542 Squadron, Benson
21-1-1944 Benson
2-2-1944   8 Operational Training Unit, Dyce
16-11-1944 Struck off charge

AB124   2297
15-11-1941 First Flight
18-11-1941 5 Maintenance Unit, Kemble
29-4-1942 Vickers-Armstrongs Ltd, Henley-on-Thames
24-7-1942 1 Photographic Reconnaissance Unit, Benson
19-10-1942 542 Squadron, Benson
9-1-1943   540 Squadron, Leuchars
20-6-1943 8 Operational Training Unit, Dyce
14-10-1943 Entered clouds on high altitude training flight, aircraft missing

AB125   2304
15-11-1941 First Flight
26-11-1941 5 Maintenance Unit, Kemble
11-12-1941 Northolt Dispersal
19-5-1942 Vickers-Armstrongs Ltd, Henley-on-Thames
8-10-1942 Benson
22-1-1943 543 Squadron, Benson, Mount Farm & St.Eval
10-2-1943 Shot down on a PR mission and crashed 10km south-west of Goes, Holland W/O E. J. Evans (k)

AB126   2298
15-11-1941 First Flight
17-11-1941 8 Maintenance Unit, Little Rissington, Gloucestershire
11-12-1941 Northolt Dispersal
14-5-1942 Vickers-Armstrongs Ltd, Henley-on-Thames
4-7-1942   140 (Tactical Air Force) Squadron, Benson
22-3-1943 Flying Accident Category.AC
           Heston Aircraft Ltd
5-1943   140 Squadron, Benson/Mount Farm
5-8-1943   Collided during formation with Spitfire AB305 and crashed Shinfield, Berkshire F/O D. M. Croy (k)

AB127   2299
15-11-1941 First Flight
18-11-1941 8 Maintenance Unit, Little Rissington
27-2-1942 Vickers-Armstrongs Ltd, Henley-on-Thames
20-4-1942 1 Photographic Reconnaissance Unit, Benson
10-5-1942 Shot down near Trondheim, Norway on a PR mission in search of the Tirpitz
           F/Lt Frederick Ian Malcolm (k)

AB128   2300
15-11-1941 First Flight
18-11-1941 8 Maintenance Unit, Little Rissington
27-2-1942 Vickers-Armstrongs Ltd, Henley-on-Thames
8-3-1942   1 Photographic Reconnaissance Unit, Benson
19-10-1942 543 Squadron, Benson, Mount Farm & St.Eval
28-2-1943 Failed to return from a PR mission to Bordeaux, France

AB129   2318
20-11-1941 First Flight
23-11-1941 8 Maintenance Unit, Little Rissington
27-2-1942   Vickers-Armstrongs Ltd, Henley-on-Thames
8-3-1942   1 Photographic Reconnaissance Unit, Benson
20-5-1942   Failed to return from a PR mission to Bordeaux, France

AB130   2325
22-11-1941 First Flight
23-11-1941 8 Maintenance Unit, Little Rissington
26-1-1942   1 Photographic Reconnaissance Unit, Benson (fitted with a Y type camera installation)
2-1942   140 Squadron, (Tactical Air Force) Benson
26-8-1942   Failed to return from a PR mission to Pontoise and Melvun, the instruments froze at 23,000 feet
            P/O A. F. Lucarotti abandoned the aircraft at 3,000 ft near East Grinstead the aircraft
            crashed near Goldstrow Farm, Newick, East Sussex, Category.E
            the remains were recovered in 1990 and on rebuild for Roger Bennington, Ludham, Norfolk
31-8-1942   Struck off charge

Spitfire PR.IV AB131.
(Peter R Arnold)

AB131   2326
22-11-1941 First Flight
7-12-1941   6 Maintenance Unit, Brize Norton
16-2-1942   1401 Meteorological Flight, Bircham Newton
1-8-1942   521 Squadron, Bircham Newton
1-9-1942   Failed to return from a Meteorological Training 'Pampa' Flight to the east coast of Ireland,
            it was blown off course due to miscalculated direction and wind force. Short of fuel, and not
            realising he was over enemy territory the pilot mistook some coal-heaps as being Wales and
            mistakenly landed at Sint-Truiden airfield near St.Trond, Belgium. P/O C. E. Heggtveit taken
            prisoner and the aircraft captured and later sent to a German Luftwaffe Flying School.

AB132   2342
26-11-1941 First Flight
30-11-1941 ? Maintenance Unit
27-1-1942   1 Photographic Reconnaissance Unit, Benson
27-2-1942   Flying accident Category.B to Heston Aircraft Ltd for repair
19-9-1942   detachment to Vaenga, North Russia for 'Operation Orator' as a replacement aircraft
23-10-1942 To VVS SF, Air Force of the Northern Fleet, Russian Air Force
10-1942   2 GAP, 2nd Guards Air Regiment
10-1942   28 OAE, 28th Independent Reconnaissance Squadron
3-1943   118 ORAP, 118th Independent Reconnaissance Aviation Regiment
4/5-1943   Possibly to (NII VVS RKKA, Scientific-Research Institute of the Air Force of the
            Workers-peasants Red Army), Akhtubinsk as '01'
5-1943?   118 ORAP, 118th Independent Reconnaissance Aviation Regiment

Spitfire PR.IV possibly AB132
marked as '01' at the NII VVS RKKA.
(K. Choloniewski via Wojtek Matusiak)

Another view of Spitfire PR.IV '01'
at the NII VVS RKKA
at Akhtubinsk in early 1943.
(P. Butowski Collection via Wojtek Matusiak)

AB300   2341
26-11-1941 First Flight
30-11-1941 5 Maintenance Unit, Kemble
17-1-1942 Benson for despatch to Middle East
1-3-1942   2 Photographic Reconnaissance Unit, Heliopolis, Egypt
7-3-1942   69 Squadron, Luqa 'B Flight'
19-9-1942 On a PR mission over Lampedusa Coast and the Sicily coast, aircraft engine lost power and
           abandoned near Agrigento, Sicily. Sgt Frank Gillions (PoW)
20-9-1942 Struck off charge

AB301   2357
30-11-1941 First Flight
5-12-1941 5 Maintenance Unit, Kemble
17-12-1942 Flying Accident Category.B Heston Aircraft Ltd for repair
5-4-1942   1 Photographic Reconnaissance Unit, Benson
30-7-1942 Missing on a PR mission to Lubeck, Germany

AB302   2358
30-11-1941 First Flight
4-12-1941 5 Maintenance Unit, Kemble
3-1-1942   1 Photographic Reconnaissance Unit, Benson
15-2-1942 Flying Accident Category.AC
19-10-1942 541 Squadron, Benson
21-6-1943 8 Operational Training Unit, Dyce
31-12-1943 Vickers-Armstrongs Supermarine Ltd external sump wing oil tank modifications
3-1944   8 Operational Training Unit, Dyce
26-3-1945 Struck off charge

AB303   2360
30-11-1941   First Flight
5-12-1941   5 Maintenance Unit, Kemble
31-1-1942   1 Photographic Reconnaissance Unit, Benson
19-10-1942 542 Squadron, Benson
9-1943   309 Ferry Training and Aircraft Despatch Unit, Benson
10-1943   542 Squadron, Benson
4-11-1943   Flying Accident Category.C
23-12-1943 Benson
7-1-1944   8 Operational Training Unit, Dyce
16-3-1945   Struck off charge

AB304   2374
5-12-1941   First Flight
7-12-1941   5 Maintenance Unit, Kemble
28-1-1942   Benson for despatch to Middle East
19-3-1942   2 Photographic Reconnaissance Unit, Heliopolis, Egypt
1-4-1942   Hit by Vickers Wellington DV517, whilst in transit at Gibraltar. Category.E

Spitfire PR.IV AB305 of 140
Squadron at Mount Farm,
Oxfordshire during 1943.
(©Hugh Rigby via Robin Rigby)

AB305   2375
5-12-1941   First Flight
7-12-1941   6 Maintenance Unit, Brize Norton
17-1-1942   1 Photographic Reconnaissance Unit, Benson (fitted with a Y type camera installation)
13-3-1942   Flying Accident Category.B on operations
3-9-1942   Heston Aircraft Ltd Merlin 46 Engine installation
16-9-1942   Flying Accident Category.A
30-9-1942   1 Photographic Reconnaissance Unit, Benson
19-10-1942 541 Squadron, Benson
24-12-1942 140 Squadron, Benson/Mount Farm
5-8-1943   Collided with Spitfire AB126 over Shinfield, Berkshire. Category.A
28-9-1943   Heston Aircraft Ltd for Merlin 45 Engine installation
5-3-1944   4 Squadron, Sawbridgeworth
15-5-1944   541 Squadron, Benson
8-12-1944   Flying accident Category.E
15-5-1945   Struck off charge

AB306   2379
6-12-1941   First Flight
7-12-1941   6 Maintenance Unit, Brize Norton
26-8-1942   Benson
14-9-1942   1 Photographic Reconnaissance Unit, Benson (fitted with W & S type camera installation)
19-10-1942 543 Squadron, Benson, Mount Farm & St.Eval
16-12-1942 Boscombe Down for trials with constant speed and de Havilland Hydromatic Propeller.
5-1-1943   521 Squadron, Bircham Newton
24-3-1943   Flying Accident Category.B
14-8-1943   1 Overseas Aircraft Delivery Unit, Portreath
7-10-1943   681 Squadron, Dum Dum, Calcutta, India
26-4-1945   Struck off charge

AB307   2394
12-12-1941 First Flight
15-12-1941 6 Maintenance Unit, Brize Norton
17-1-1942   1 Photographic Reconnaissance Unit, Benson (detachment at Wick)
10-4-1942   Shot down by a Bf109 over Lake Hammervatnet, Norway on a PR Flight to Trondheim
                    to photograph the *Tirpitz* F/O Peter Geoffrey Charles Gimson baled out but was killed
Total Flying Hours 38

AB308   2395
12-12-1941 First Flight
15-12-1941 6 Maintenance Unit, Brize Norton
19-9-1942   1 Photographic Reconnaissance Unit, Benson
11-1942   Royal Aircraft Establishment, Farnborough for Photo trials
21-2-1943   543 Squadron, Benson, Mount Farm & St.Eval
6-9-1943   Flying Accident Category.AC
7-1-1944   8 Operational Training Unit, Dyce
16-3-1945   Struck off charge

AB309   2401
15-12-1941 First Flight
17-12-1941 6 Maintenance Unit, Brize Norton
9-3-1942   1 Photographic Reconnaissance Unit, Benson
19-10-1942 541 Squadron, Benson
6-11-1942   Believed to have been shot down by flak near Caen, France on a PR mission to Cherbourg

AB310   2402
16-12-1941 First Flight
23-12-1941 9 Maintenance Unit, Cosford, Shropshire
13-1-1943   Benson
13-2-1943   1 Overseas Aircraft Delivery Unit, Portreath
23-2-1943   683 Squadron, Luqa, Malta
                    680 Squadron, Heliopolis (detachments to Nicosia)
1-7-1943   680 Squadron, Nicosia, Cyprus
4-9-1943   Crashed on landing Nicosia

AB311   2405
18-12-1941 First Flight
19-12-1941 Maintenance Unit
                    1 Photographic Reconnaissance Unit, Benson
19-10-1942 542 Squadron, Benson
5-1943   1 Overseas Aircraft Delivery Unit, Portreath
                    681 Squadron, Dum Dum, Calcutta India (aircraft coded 'R')
26-4-1945   Struck off charge

AB312   2426
23-12-1941 First Flight
27-12-1941 Maintenance Unit
9-3-1942   1 Photographic Reconnaissance Unit, Benson
17-3-1942   2 Photographic Reconnaissance Unit, Heliopolis, Egypt
19-10-1942 Missing in action

AB313   2446
29-12-1941 First Flight
2-1-1942   9 Maintenance Unit, Cosford
13-1-1942   Royal Aircraft Establishment, Farnborough, Camera and Instrument Trials
30-3-1943   Whilst doing low-level circuits the aircraft was caught by a severe downdraught and one
            wing hit a hut, the aircraft crashed and was burnt out at Benson. S/L R. V. Whitehead DFC (k)

AB314   2427
25-12-1941 First Flight
29-12-1941 9 Maintenance Unit, Cosford
3-5-1942   1 Photographic Reconnaissance Unit, Benson
4-8-1942   Damaged by flak and crashed Funäsdalen, Sweden on a PR mission to Trondheim, Norway
            F/Lt Leslie Whitaker baled out and interned, the wreckage was stripped by locals and the
            remains of the aircraft were taken to Froson and later scrapped

AB315   2428
25-12-1941 First Flight
29-12-1941 12 Maintenance Unit, Kirkbride, Cumbria
10-2-1943   1 Photographic Reconnaissance Unit, Benson
18-3-1943   1 Overseas Aircraft Delivery Unit, Portreath
27-3-1943   680 Squadron, Heliopolis, Egypt
10-4-1943   681 Squadron, Dum Dum, Calcutta India (aircraft coded 'H')
1-5-1943   Middle East
31-8-1944   Struck off charge

AB316   2438
28-12-1941 First Flight
29-12-1941 12 Maintenance Unit, Kirkbride
20-3-1943   Benson
5-6-1943   681 Squadron, Dum Dum, Calcutta India (aircraft coded 'D')
15-12-1943 Failed to return from a PR mission to Mandalay, Burma. F/O Gordon-White (PoW)

AB317   2447
29-12-1941 First Flight
3-1-1942   12 Maintenance Unit, Kirkbride
8-4-1942   1 Photographic Reconnaissance Unit, Benson (fitted with a Y camera)
28-8-1942   Failed to return from a PR mission to Bergen, Norway

AB318   2458
2-1-1942   First Flight
3-1-1942   12 Maintenance Unit, Kirkbride
13-1-1943   Benson
27-2-1943   1 Overseas Aircraft Delivery Unit, Portreath
1-4-1943   681 Squadron, Dum Dum, Calcutta India
8-6-1943   Returning from mission to Lashio and Loiwing, flew into a thunderstorm over the Ganges Delta
            and broke-up due to severe gale force winds, Talliagi-Cha, Burma. W/O F.D.C. Brown baling out

* Uncertain if assembled at Henley

AB319   2450
31-12-1941 First Flight
3-1-1942   12 Maintenance Unit, Kirkbride
13-1-1943 Benson
27-2-1943 1 Overseas Aircraft Delivery Unit, Portreath
1-4-1943   681 Squadron, Dum Dum, Calcutta India (aircraft coded 'J')
30-7-1943 On a mission to Meiktila, Burma force-landed near Alethangwin airstrip. Sgt P. S. Marman
           The aircraft was impossible to recover so was destroyed by dive-bombers of 45 Squadron

*AB421   2459
1-1-1942   First Flight
3-1-1942   6 Maintenance Unit, Brize Norton
27-1-1942 1 Photographic Reconnaissance Unit, Benson
17-3-1942 2 Photographic Reconnaissance Unit, Heliopolis, Egypt
13-10-1942 Flying Accident on operations
2-1943   680 Squadron, Heliopolis, Egypt
           74 Operational Training Unit, Aqir/Petah Tiqva
3-3-1945   Swung on landing and overturned Petah Tiqva
29-3-1945 Struck off charge

AB422   2469
6-1-1942   First Flight
12-1-1942 6 Maintenance Unit, Brize Norton
17-2-1942 1 Photographic Reconnaissance Unit, Benson (fitted with a Y type camera installation)
28-8-1942 Shot down 40km West of Helgoland, Germany on a PR mission to Kassel, Sgt F. C. Evans (k)

AB423   2470
7-1-1942   First Flight
9-1-1942   6 Maintenance Unit, Brize Norton
13-9-1942 1 Photographic Reconnaissance Unit, Benson (fitted with a W camera)
19-10-1942 543 Squadron, Benson, Mount Farm & St.Eval
3-9-1943   543 Squadron, Vaenga, Northern Russia arrived 4-9 'Operation Source'
1-11-1943 118 ORAP, 118th Independent Reconnaissance Aviation Regiment, Russia
5-12-1943 Struck off RAF charge

AB424   2480
9-1-1942   First Flight
12-1-1942 6 Maintenance Unit, Brize Norton
28-2-1942 1 Photographic Reconnaissance Unit, Benson
19-10-1942 543 Squadron, Benson/Mount Farm
3-9-1943   Heston Aircraft Ltd for modifications
19-10-1943 Flying accident Category.AC
11-1943   309 Ferry Training and Aircraft Despatch Unit, Benson
20-2-1945 Over-ran runway and undercarriage collapsed Benson

AB425   2481
9-1-1942   First Flight
11-1-1942 6 Maintenance Unit, Brize Norton
28-2-1942 1 Photographic Reconnaissance Unit, Benson
23-4-1942 Failed to return from a PR mission to Emden, Germany, crashed Wadden Zee off Ameland, Holland
           F/Sgt C. M. T. Rogers

* Uncertain if assembled at Henley

*AB426   2524
25-1-1942 First Flight
28-1-1942 8 Maintenance Unit, Little Rissington
27-2-1942 1 Photographic Reconnaissance Unit, Benson
4-10-1942 Flying Accident Category.AC
19-12-1942 541 Squadron, Benson
25-1-1943 1 Overseas Aircraft Delivery Unit, Portreath
26-1-1943 Flying Accident Category.AC
28-2-1943 682 Squadron, Maison Blanche, Algiers, Algeria
30-9-1943 To Middle East
30-11-1943 218 Group, North Africa
30-11-1944 Struck off charge

*AB427   2525
25-1-1942 First Flight
28-1-1942 8 Maintenance Unit, Little Rissington
27-2-1942 1 Photographic Reconnaissance Unit, Benson
30-9-1942 543 Squadron, Benson, Mount Farm & St.Eval
3-9-1943 543 Squadron, Vaenga, Northern Russia arrived 4-9 'Operation Source'
1-11-1943 118 ORAP, 118th Independent Reconnaissance Aviation Regiment, Russia
5-12-1943 Struck off RAF charge

*AB428   2526
25-1-1942 First Flight
28-1-1942 8 Maintenance Unit, Little Rissington
24-8-1942 Benson
3-9-1942 1 Photographic Reconnaissance Unit, Benson (fitted with a W type camera installation)
24-9-1942 Flying Accident Category.B
19-10-1942 541 Squadron, Benson
5-3-1943 Flying Accident Category.B on operations
9-9-1943 1 Overseas Aircraft Delivery Unit, Portreath
10-10-1943 216 Group Communication Flight, India
31-5-1945 Struck off charge

*AB429   2528
26-1-1942 First Flight
30-1-1942 8 Maintenance Unit, Little Rissington
28-2-1942 1 Photographic Reconnaissance Unit, Benson
26-3-1942 Engine failed and aircraft overshot the runway and tipped onto it's nose on landing South Marston
          Scottish Aviation Ltd, Prestwick
          Struck off charge

*AB430   2529
26-1-1942 First Flight
7-2-1942 8 Maintenance Unit, Little Rissington
27-2-1942 1 Photographic Reconnaissance Unit, Benson
19-10-1942 542 Squadron, Benson
26-1-1943 Failed to return from a PR mission to Ghent, Belguim

Contract No. B19713/39 Fifth order

*BP879   2539?
28-1-1942   First Flight
30-1-1942   9 Maintenance Unit, Cosford
29-8-1942   Benson
22-10-1942 541 Squadron, Benson (fitted with a W type camera installation)
9-5-1943   Heston Aircraft Ltd for modifications
19-5-1943   542 Squadron, Benson
7-7-1943   543 Squadron, Benson/Mount Farm
18-10-1943 309 Ferry Training and Aircraft Despatch Unit, Benson
5-11-1943   Engine failed on take-off and aircraft made a wheels-up landing Benson. Category.E

*BP880   2551
31-1-1942   First Flight
6-2-1942   1 Photographic Reconnaissance Unit, Benson
16-3-1942   Crashed on route to the Middle East
20-6-1942   Heston Aircraft Ltd for repair
13-1-1943   Benson
23-9-1943   681 Squadron, Dum Dum, Calcutta India (coded'S' "The Flying Scotsman")
5-3-1944   Aircraft broke-up and was abandoned over Bay of Bengal. F/Lt C. B. P. Davies (missing)

*BP881   2540
28-1-1942   First Flight
30-1-1942   9 Maintenance Unit, Cosford
28-8-1942   Benson
1-9-1942   1 Photographic Reconnaissance Unit, Benson (fitted with a W type camera installation)
19-10-1942 541 Squadron, Benson
8-2-1943   Failed to return from a PR mission to Hook, Rotterdam, Terneuzen and Antwerp
              S/L Van Der Heyden (missing)

*BP882   2552
31-1-1942   First Flight
6-2-1942   1 Photographic Reconnaissance Unit, Benson
17-3-1942   2 Photographic Reconnaissance Unit, Heliopolis, Egypt
1-2-1943   680 Squadron, Heliopolis
1-4-1943   Ran out of fuel and force-landed in Turkey Category.E

*BP883   2553
31-1-1942   First Flight
6-2-1942   1 Photographic Reconnaissance Unit, Benson
17-3-1942   2 Photographic Reconnaissance Unit, Heliopolis, Egypt
6-9-1942   Malta
22-9-1942   Missing Crete

*BP884   2561
7-2-1942   First Flight
15-2-1942   8 Maintenance Unit, Little Rissington
3-5-1942   1 Photographic Reconnaissance Unit, Benson
19-10-1942 542 Squadron, Benson
18-6-1943   Heston Aircraft Ltd for Merlin 45 engine installation
23-2-1944   Benson
7-3-1944   542 Squadron, Benson detachment to Vaenga, Russia 'Operation Tungsten'
              to Soviet Air Force

Spitfire PR.IV possibly BP885 fitted with a
Tropical Filter seen here in Malta and
believed flown by F/Lt Adrian Warburton.
(Bill Costin via Peter R Arnold)

*BP885	2562
7-2-1942	First Flight
15-2-1942	8 Maintenance Unit, Little Rissington
14-3-1942	1 Photographic Reconnaissance Unit, Benson
3-1942	2 Photographic Reconnaissance Unit, Heliopolis, Egypt (commandeered on Malta & not delivered)
19-3-1942	69 Squadron, Luqa, Malta 'B Flight'
1943	680 Squadron
13-9-1945	Struck off charge

BP886	2550
10-2-1942	First Flight
14-2-1942	8 Maintenance Unit, Little Rissington
27-2-1942	1 Photographic Reconnaissance Unit, Benson
19-10-1942	542 Squadron, Benson
3-6-1943	8 Operational Training Unit, Dyce
8-9-1943	Vickers-Armstrongs Supermarine Ltd for external sump wing oil tank modifications
11-1943	8 Operational Training Unit, Dyce
25-4-1944	Flying accident Category.AC repaired on site
23-4-1945	Struck off charge

BP887	2581
11-2-1942	First Flight
13-2-1942	8 Maintenance Unit, Little Rissington
24-2-1942	Controller of Research & Development, Farnborough
18-4-1942	1 Photographic Reconnaissance Unit, Benson (fitted with a W type camera installation)
17-8-1942	Failed to return from a PR mission to Hamburg, Bremen and Bremerhaven, Germany

Spitfire PR.IV BP888. (V. Flintham Collection)

BP888   2582
11-2-1942   First Flight
14-2-1942   8 Maintenance Unit, Little Rissington
22-8-1942   Benson
28-8-1942   Flying Accident Category.B to Heston Aircraft Ltd for repair
3-9-1942   Benson
5-1943   Aeroplane & Armament Experimental Establishment, Boscombe Down
10-9-1943   8 Operational Training Unit, Dyce
27-10-1944 Swung on landing and undercarriage collapsed, Dyce. Category.E

BP890   2608
21-2-1942   First Flight
22-2-1942   1 Photographic Reconnaissance Unit, Benson
18-3-1942   Crashed on Ferry Flight to the Middle East

BP892   2600
21-2-1942   First Flight
22-2-1942   1 Photographic Reconnaissance Unit, Benson
19-3-1942   2 Photographic Reconnaissance Unit, Heliopolis, Egypt
1-4-1942   Hit by Vickers Wellington DV517, whilst in transit at Gibraltar. Category.E

BP904   2610
21-2-1942   First Flight
22-2-1942   1 Photographic Reconnaissance Unit, Benson
17-3-1942   2 Photographic Reconnaissance Unit, Heliopolis, Egypt
23-9-1942   Flying accident
1-2-1943   680 Squadron, Heliopolis, Egypt
           74 Operational Training Unit, Aqir/Petah Tiqva, Palestine
23-1-1945   Engine cut and aircraft overshot and belly-landed then overturned Qastina

BP905   2616
23-2-1942   First Flight
25-2-1942   1 Photographic Reconnaissance Unit, Benson
3-1942   1 Overseas Aircraft Delivery Unit, Portreath
1-4-1942   Flying accident Category.B on ferry flight to Malta
24-4-1942   Ferry flight to UK to Heston Aircraft Ltd
27-11-1942 Benson
7-12-1942   69 Squadron, Luqa, Malta 'B Flight'
8-2-1943   683 Squadron, Luqa
1-4-1943   682 Squadron, Maison Blanche, Algiers, Algeria
1-6-1943   North Africa PR Wing
1-7-1943   74 Operational Training Unit, Petah Tiqva, Palestine
30-11-1944 Struck off charge

BP906   2623
27-2-1942   First Flight
7-3-1942   1 Photographic Reconnaissance Unit, Benson
29-3-1942   2 Photographic Reconnaissance Unit, Heliopolis, Egypt
1-4-1942   Force-landed in neutral French North-West Africa, on route to the Middle East
30-4-1942   Struck off charge
Total Flying Hours 9.20

BP907   2624
27-2-1942   First Flight
7-3-1942   1 Photographic Reconnaissance Unit, Benson
4-1942   Royal Aircraft Establishment, Farnborough, camera trials
20-4-1942   Force-landed and interned in Tunisia whilst on a ferry flight to the Middle East, via Gibraltar
            and Malta for delivery to 2 Photographic Reconnaissance Unit, Heliopolis
Total Flying Hours 8.30

BP908   2633
28-2-1942   First Flight
7-3-1942   1 Photographic Reconnaissance Unit, Benson
14-4-1942   2 Photographic Reconnaissance Unit, Heliopolis, Egypt
            (commandeered on Malta & not delivered)
6-1942   69 Squadron, Luqa, Malta 'B Flight'
8-3-1946   Struck off charge

BP909   2645
7-3-1942   First Flight
8-3-1942   1 Photographic Reconnaissance Unit, Benson
5-4-1942   2 Photographic Reconnaissance Unit, Heliopolis, Egypt
1-2-1943   680 Squadron, Heliopolis, Egypt
            74 Operational Training Unit, Petah Tiqva, Palestine
1-2-1944   Struck off charge

BP910   2646
7-3-1942   First Flight
12-3-1942   6 Maintenance Unit, Brize Norton
1-5-1942   Benson, Ferry flight to the Middle East
            2 Photographic Reconnaissance Unit, Heliopolis, Egypt
8-2-1943   683 Squadron, Luqa, Malta
13-3-1943   Struck off charge

BP911   2655
8-3-1942   First Flight
12-3-1942   6 Maintenance Unit, Brize Norton
12-4-1942   Benson, Ferry flight to the Middle East
4-1942   2 Photographic Reconnaissance Unit, Heliopolis, Egypt
11-8-1942   69 Squadron, Luqa, Malta 'B Flight'
10-10-1942 Arrived at Karachi, Western Pakistan via Egypt
10-1942   3 Photographic Reconnaissance Unit, Dum Dum, Calcutta, India
25-1-1943   681 Squadron, Dum Dum (aircraft coded 'T')
26-4-1945   Struck off charge

BP912   2672
14-3-1942   First Flight
15-3-1942   6 Maintenance Unit, Brize Norton
17-3-1942   Benson
4-1942   1 Overseas Aircraft Delivery Unit, Portreath
17-4-1942   Overshot on Landing at Portreath and hit a wall Category.E
18-5-1942   Benson
31-8-1942   47 Maintenance Unit, Sealand, Cheshire
3-10-1942   Aircraft lost at sea onboard ship 'Molaja' on route to the Middle East

BP913   2670
13-3-1942   First Flight
15-3-1942   6 Maintenance Unit, Brize Norton
6-5-1942   Benson, Ferry flight to the Middle East
4-1942   1 Overseas Aircraft Delivery Unit, Portreath
6-5-1942   2 Photographic Reconnaissance Unit, Heliopolis, Egypt
1-2-1943   680 Squadron, Heliopolis
15-4-1943   Suffered a glycol leak and crashed landed on Djerba Island, Tunisia
1-6-1943   Struck off charge

BP914   2698
14-3-1942   First Flight
25-3-1942   1 Photographic Reconnaissance Unit, Benson
3-5-1942   69 Squadron, Luqa, Malta 'B Flight'
4-5-1942   Flying accident Category.A on operations
            2 Photographic Reconnaissance Unit, Heliopolis, Egypt
6-8-1942   Missing over Mersa Matruh, Egypt

BP915
20-3-1942   First Flight
3-1942   1 Photographic Reconnaissance Unit, Benson
5-1942   69 Squadron, Luqa, Malta 'B Flight'
            2 Photographic Reconnaissance Unit, Heliopolis, Egypt
1-2-1943   680 Squadron, Helipolis, Egypt
5-2-1943   Aircraft damaged beyond repair in an accident

BP916   2707
20-3-1942   First Flight
25-3-1942   1 Photographic Reconnaissance Unit, Benson
5-6-1942   2 Photographic Reconnaissance Unit, Heliopolis, Egypt
17-6-1942   Shot down by Bf109 flown by Hans-Joachim Marseille on a mission from Sidi Barrani, Egypt
            P/O Squires

BP917   2720
25-3-1942   First Flight
26-3-1942   8 Maintenance Unit, Little Rissington
30-4-1942   1 Photographic Reconnaissance Unit, Benson
31-5-1942   Flying accident Category.E
19-10-1942 543 Squadron, Benson, Mount Farm & St.Eval
30-6-1943   Heston Aircraft Ltd for modifications
23-2-1944   Benson
7-3-1944   542 Squadron, Vaenga, Russia 'Operation Tungsten'
            to Soviet Air Force

BP918   2708
23-3-1942   First Flight
24-3-1942   8 Maintenance Unit, Little Rissington
3-8-1942   1 Photographic Reconnaissance Unit, Benson
19-10-1942 542 Squadron, Benson
20-6-1943   8 Operational Training Unit, Dyce
11-10-1944 Undercarriage jammed and aircraft belly-landed, Dyce. Category.AC re: Category.E

BP919   2709
23-3-1942 First Flight
27-3-1942 9 Maintenance Unit, Cosford
14-5-1942 1401 Meteorological Flight, Bircham Newton
14-6-1942 1 Photographic Reconnaissance Unit, Benson
19-10-1942 541 Squadron, Benson
24-12-1942 140 Squadron, Benson (detachments at Mount Farm, St.Eval, Weston Zoyland)
14-4-1943 Flying accident Category.AC
26-6-1943 140 Squadron, Hartford Bridge, Hampshire
31-3-1945 2 Satellite Landing Ground (39 MU), Starveall Farm near Wootton, Oxfordshire for storage
4-4-1945   Struck off charge

BP920   2727
26-3-1942 First Flight
30-3-1942 9 Maintenance Unit, Cosford
5-12-1942 Benson
4-1-1943   47 Maintenance Unit, Sealand
1-8-1943   680 Squadron, Heliopolis, Egypt
           74 Operational Training Unit, Aqir/Petah Tiqva, Palestine
3-4-1945   Collided with North American Harvard EZ340 at Petah Tiqva
31-5-1945 Struck off charge

BP921   2744
28-3-1942 First Flight
30-3-1942 9 Maintenance Unit, Cosford
3-5-1942   1 Photographic Reconnaissance Unit, Benson
18-7-1942 On a sortie to Flensburg (U-Boat yards), Germany diverted to Coltishall due to bad weather,
           returned to Benson but crashed in low cloud whilst following a railway line near Duxford.
           F/L A. F. P. Fane (k)
31-7-1942 Struck off charge

BP922   2734
27-3-1942 First Flight
30-3-1942 9 Maintenance Unit, Cosford
5-5-1942   1 Photographic Reconnaissance Unit, Benson
19-10-1942 541 Squadron, Benson
29-10-1942 Flying accident Category.AC to Heston Aircraft Ltd for repair
13-11-1942 415 Squadron, Thorney Island, Hampshire
24-11-1942 140 Squadron, Benson (detachments at Mount Farm, St.Eval, Weston Zoyland)
1-7-1943   74 Operational Training Unit, Petah Tiqva, Palestine
18-12-1943 Crashed during a forced-landing whilst lost over Genosar near Lake Tiberias, Palestine
1-2-1944   Struck off charge

Peter Arnold with a piece of the recovered
BP923 showing part of the Russian 'Red Star'
Insignia in 1992. (Peter R Arnold)

The wreckage of Spitfire PR.IV BP923 at Gardermoen, Norway in 1990. (Peter R Arnold)

BP923   2741 & 6S/138536
28-3-1942 First Flight
30-3-1942 9 Maintenance Unit, Cosford
5-5-1942   1 Photographic Reconnaissance Unit, Benson
1-9-1942   1 PRU, detachment to Vaenga, Northern Russia arrived 2-9 used on 'Operation Orator'
23-10-1942 To VVS SF, Air Force of the Northern Fleet, Russian Air Force
10-1942   2 GAP, 2nd Guards Air Regiment
10-1942   28 OAE, 28th Independent Reconnaissance Squadron
3-1943   3 Eskadrilyas, 118 ORAP, 118th Independent Reconnaissance Aviation Regiment, Russia
4-9-1943   Failed to return from a PR mission to Altafjord/Kaafjord, Norway, shot down by German
              fighters and crashed into the side of Vad'dasgaissa mountain near lake Levnasjavvre
              Senior Lieutenant Vladimir N Solovkin (k)
9-1989   Aircraft recovered and taken to Royal Norwegian Air Force Museum, Gardermoen
12-2000   Under restoration by Sven Kindblom, Sollen Tuna near Stockholm, Sweden

BP924   2762
1-4-1942   First Flight
3-4-1942   5 Maintenance Unit, Kemble
16-4-1942   1 Photographic Reconnaissance Unit, Benson (fitted with a X type camera installation)
28-8-1942   Failed to return from a PR mission to Cuxhaven, Germany

BP925   2763
1-4-1942   First Flight
3-4-1942   5 Maintenance Unit, Kemble
13-4-1942   Royal Aircraft Establishment, Farnborough for photo-trials
8-1942   Aeroplane & Armament Experimental Establishment, Boscombe Down
19-9-1942   33 Maintenance Unit, Lyneham, Wiltshire
27-10-1942 Benson
9-12-1942   8 Operational Training Unit, Fraserburgh
9-3-1943   Flying accident Category.AC to Heston Aircraft Ltd for repair
19-8-1943   Benson
3-9-1943   544 Squadron, Gibraltar 'Operation Torch'
14-9-1943   Flying accident Category.AC
17-10-1943 541 Squadron, Benson
3-4-1944   Benson
10-9-1944   Station Flight, Gibraltar
31-10-1946 Struck off charge

BP926   2770 & 6S/171374
2-4-1942   First Flight
3-4-1942   5 Maintenance Unit, Kemble
19-5-1942   1 Photographic Reconnaissance Unit, Benson
25-9-1942   Flying accident Category.A
31-10-1942 542 Squadron, Benson
4-1943   8 Operational Training Unit, Dyce
28-5-1943   Flying accident Category.A
22-6-1943   Heston Aircraft Ltd
18-2-1944   106 Photo Reconnaissance Wing, Benson
7-3-1944   542 Squadron, Vaenga, Northern Russia 'Operation Tungsten' to Soviet Air Force
            Wreck recovered from Norway (see page 91)
14-4-2010   Registered as G-PRIV to Peter R. Arnold

BP927   2775
3-4-1942   First Flight
3-4-1942   6 Maintenance Unit, Brize Norton
17-5-1942   Vickers-Armstrongs Ltd for Merlin 45 Installation
            Benson
31-10-1942 543 Squadron, Benson, Mount Farm & St.Eval (fitted with a W type camera installation)
22-10-1943 8 Operational Training Unit, Dyce
31-8-1944   Overshot on landing Dyce. Category.B re: Category.E 23-9-1944

BP928   2776
3-4-1942   First Flight
3-4-1942   5 Maintenance Unit, Kemble
14-5-1942   1401 Meteorological Flight, Bircham Newton
31-12-1942 521 Squadron, Bircham Newton
5-4-1943   Benson
7-5-1943   680 Squadron, Heliopolis, Egypt
8-7-1943   Engine cut-out and aircraft abandoned over the sea 78 miles West of Sidon, Lebanon
            Capt D. R. C. Main SAAF (k)

BP929   2794
10-4-1942   First Flight
13-4-1942   38 Maintenance Unit, Llandow, Glamorgan
19-5-1942   1 Photographic Reconnaissance Unit, Benson (fitted with a W type camera installation)
10-9-1942   Flying accident Category.B on operations
17-11-1942 543 Squadron, Benson/Mount Farm
25-5-1943   8 Operational Training Unit, Dyce
26-8-1943   Flying accident Category.AC
            Heston Aircraft Ltd for Merlin 46 Installation
18-2-1944   106 Photographic Reconnaissance Wing, Benson
7-3-1944   542 Squadron, Vaenga, Northern Russia 'Operation Tungsten'
            to Soviet Air Force

BP930   2808
11-4-1942   First Flight
13-4-1942   38 Maintenance Unit, Llandow
28-11-1942 Benson
12-1942   1 Overseas Aircraft Delivery Unit, Portreath
25-12-1942 4 Photographic Reconnaissance Unit, Gibraltar
28-12-1942 4 Photographic Reconnaissance Unit, Maison Blanche, Algiers, Algeria
1-2-1943   682 Squadron, Maison Blanche
1-1-1947   Struck off charge

BP931   2796
10-4-1942   First Flight
13-4-1942   38 Maintenance Unit, Llandow
14-5-1942   1401 Meteorological Flight, Bircham Newton
28-8-1942   Flying Accident Category.AC
31-12-1942 521 Squadron, Bircham Newton
1-4-1943   1401 Meteorological Flight, Bircham Newton
16-9-1943   Heston Aircraft Ltd for Merlin 46 Installation
27-1-1945   8 Operational Training Unit, Haverfordwest, Pembrokeshire
21-8-1945   Struck off charge to Maintenance Command as 4992M

BP932   2818
14-4-1942   First Flight
16-4-1942   38 Maintenance Unit, Llandow
27-11-1942 Benson
12-1942   1 Overseas Aircraft Delivery Unit, Portreath
19-12-1942 69 Squadron, Luqa, Malta 'B Flight'
8-2-1943   683 Squadron, Luqa, Malta
1-9-1943   680 Squadron, Heliopolis, Egypt
31-5-1945   Struck off charge

BP933   2819
15-4-1942   First Flight
18-4-1942   1 Photographic Reconnaissance Unit, Benson
5-6-1942   2 Photographic Reconnaissance Unit, Heliopolis, Egypt
28-6-1942   Flying accident Category.B
26-10-1942 Failed to return from Operations

BP934   2831
16-4-1942   First Flight
18-4-1942   1 Photographic Reconnaissance Unit, Benson
25-5-1942   47 Maintenance Unit, Sealand
16-6-1942   'Corabella' by sea to Takoradi, Gold Coast arrived 30-7-1942
11-8-1942   2 Photographic Reconnaissance Unit, Heliopolis, Egypt
13-10-1942 Failed to return from Operations

BP935   2832
17-4-1942   First Flight
18-4-1942   1 Photographic Reconnaissance Unit, Benson
25-5-1942   45 Maintenance Unit, Kinloss, Moray
16-6-1942   'Corabella' by sea to Takoradi, Gold Coast arrived 30-7-1942
11-8-1942   2 Photographic Reconnaissance Unit, Heliopolis, Egypt
10-10-1942 3 Photographic Reconnaissance Unit, Dum Dum, Calcutta, India
6-11-1942   Category.AC accident
25-1-1943   681 Squadron, Dum Dum (aircraft coded 'Y')
2-8-1943   Struck off charge

BP936   2841
18-4-1942   First Flight
19-4-1942   1 Photographic Reconnaissance Unit, Benson
23-5-1942   47 Maintenance Unit, Sealand
16-6-1942   'Corabella' by sea to Takoradi, Gold Coast arrived 30-7-1942
11-8-1942   2 Photographic Reconnaissance Unit, Helopolis, Egypt
1-2-1943   680 Squadron, Heliopolis, Egypt
            Aboukir Station Flight, Egypt
30-9-1943   Gibraltar
5-4-1945   Struck off charge

BP937   2872
29-4-1942   First Flight
1-5-1942   6 Maintenance Unit, Brize Norton
29-8-1942   1 Photographic Reconnaissance Unit, Benson (fitted with a W type camera installation)
19-10-1942 541 Squadron, Benson
16-8-1943   Benson
9-10-1943   681 Squadron, Dum Dum, Calcutta, India (aircraft coded 'N')
26-3-1945   Struck off charge

Spitfire PR.IV(T)

BR410   2842
18-4-1942   First Flight
19-4-1942   1 Photographic Reconnaissance Unit, Benson
30-5-1942   Flying Accident Category.AC to Heston Aircraft Ltd for repair
6-1942   1 Overseas Aircraft Delivery Unit, Portreath
18-6-1942   2 Photographic Reconnaissance Unit, Helopolis, Egypt
1-2-1943   680 Squadron, RAF Heliopolis, Egypt
            74 Operational Training Unit, Petah Tiqva, Palestine
15-12-1943 Hit a pylon and crashed near Athanya, Palestine

BR411   2843
18-4-1942   First Flight
19-4-1942   1 Photographic Reconnaissance Unit, Benson
5-1942   1 Overseas Aircraft Delivery Unit, Portreath
5-6-1942   2 Photographic Reconnaissance Unit, Helopolis, Egypt
4-10-1942 Missing on operations, Crete

BR412   2874
30-4-1942   First Flight
2-5-1942   6 Maintenance Unit, Brize Norton
13-5-1942   39 Maintenance Unit, Colerne, Wiltshire
19-10-1942 543 Squadron, Benson, Mount Farm & St.Eval (fitted with a Y type camera installation)
10-11-1943 309 Ferry Training and Aircraft Despatch Unit, Benson
13-3-1945   Swung off runway during landing and undercarriage collapsed
26-3-1945   Struck off charge

BR413   2865
24-4-1942   Swung on take-off and crashed whilst avoiding a Miles Magister, Henley
            Vickers-Supermarine, production test pilot Lt John Peter Wakefield (k)

BR414   2869
25-4-1942   First Flight
30-4-1942   1 Photographic Reconnaissance Unit, Benson
26-5-1942   47 Maintenance Unit, Sealand
16-6-1942   'Corabella' by sea to Takoradi, Gold Coast arrived 30-7-1942
8-11-1942   2 Photographic Reconnaissance Unit, Heliopolis, Egypt
4-1-1943   Flying accident on operations
1-2-1943   680 Squadron, Heliopolis
24-10-1943 Flew into a hill near Bodrum, Turkey

BR415   2891
2-5-1942   First Flight
3-5-1942   6 Maintenance Unit, Brize Norton
8-6-1942   1 Photographic Reconnaissance Unit, Benson (fitted with a W type camera installation)
14-9-1942   Flying accident Category. B on operations
16-11-1942 544 Squadron, Gibraltar
9-3-1943   541 Squadron, Benson
13-4-1943   Flying accident Category.B to Heston Aircraft Ltd for repair
25-4-1943   Benson
3-9-1943   681 Squadron, Dum Dum, Calcutta, India (aircraft coded 'T')
29-1-1944   Control of aircraft lost in clouds and crashed 10 miles South of Batachara, Bengal, India

Spitfire PR.IV BR416 with an Aboukir filter at Marble Arch, Northern Algeria in January 1943 with pilot Capt. 'Jerry' Orr. (Steve McLean via Peter R Arnold)

Spitfire PR.IV BR416 'X' this time at 74 OTU, Petah Tiqva, Palestine. (Peter R Arnold)

BR416	2871
28-4-1942	First Flight
2-5-1942	1 Photographic Reconnaissance Unit, Benson
13-7-1942	47 Maintenance Unit, Sealand
22-7-1942	'Amot Elkirk' by sea to Takoradi, Gold Coast arrived 3-9-1942
19-10-1942	2 Photographic Reconnaissance Unit, Heliopolis, Egypt
1-1943	(1437 Strategic Reconnaissance Fight, Marble Arch)?
1-2-1943	680 Squadron, Heliopolis, Egypt
1944	74 Operational Training Unit, Petah Tiqva, Palestine (aircraft coded 'X')
13-9-1945	Struck off charge

BR417	2892
2-5-1942	First Flight
3-5-1942	6 Maintenance Unit, Brize Norton
15-6-1942	1 Photographic Reconnaissance Unit, Benson
30-7-1942	Flying accident Category.B on operations
13-1-1943	Benson
17-2-1943	Flew in to high ground in cloud 2 miles South-East of Camborne, Cornwall on delivery to the 1 Overseas Aircraft Delivery Unit, Portreath. Sgt John J. McCrohan (k)

BR418	2914
8-5-1942	First Flight
10-5-1942	9 Maintenance Unit, Cosford
17-9-1942	Benson
3-10-1942	47 Maintenance Unit, Sealand
20-11-1942	'Catrine' by sea to Takoradi, Gold Coast arrived 27-12-1942
	680 Squadron, Heliopolis, Egypt
1-2-1943	681 Squadron, Dum Dum, Calcutta, India
31-8-1944	Struck off charge

BR419   2920
9-5-1942   First Flight
10-5-1942   9 Maintenance Unit, Cosford
26-5-1942   1 Photographic Reconnaissance Unit, Benson
2-8-1942   Flying accident Category.B on operations
31-10-1942 543 Squadron, Benson, Mount Farm & St.Eval
20-10-1943 8 Operational Training Unit, Dyce
31-12-1943 Failed to return from a training flight
Total Flying Hours 172.5

BR420   2921
9-5-1942   First Flight
10-5-1942   9 Maintenance Unit, Cosford
30-5-1942   1 Photographic Reconnaissance Unit, Benson
17-9-1942   to Takoradi, Gold Coast
19-9-1942   2 Photographic Reconnaissance Unit, Heliopolis
12-1943   680 Squadron, Matariya
12-3-1945   Struck off charge

BR421   2928
11-5-1942   First Flight
13-5-1942   9 Maintenance Unit, Cosford
5-10-1942   Benson
28-2-1943   682 Squadron, Maison Blanche, Algiers, Algeria
3-8-1945   Struck off charge

BR422   2947
15-5-1942   First Flight
18-5-1942   9 Maintenance Unit, Cosford
27-9-1942   1 Photographic Reconnaissance Unit, Benson (fitted with a Y type camera installation)
2-11-1942   8 Operational Training Unit, Fraserburgh
11-1943   Vickers-Armstrongs Supermarine Ltd for external sump wing oil tank modifications
1-44   8 Operational Training Unit, Dyce
22-5-1945   Struck off charge

BR423   2936
15-5-1942   First Flight
16-5-1942   9 Maintenance Unit, Cosford
2-9-1942   Benson
10-1942   1 Overseas Aircraft Delivery Unit, Portreath
6-11-1942   4 Photographic Reconnaissance Unit, Gibraltar
13-11-1942 4 Photographic Reconnaissance Unit, Maison Blanche, Algiers, Algeria
31-12-1942 Missing on Operations, Kairouan, Tunisia

BR424   2984
16-5-1942   First Flight
19-5-1942   9 Maintenance Unit, Cosford
7-9-1942   Benson
11-10-1942 47 Maintenance Unit, Sealand
31-10-1942 1 Overseas Aircraft Delivery Unit, Portreath
6-11-1942   to Malta
29-1-1943   Missing on operations. Category.E
1-2-1943   Struck off charge

BR425   2949
16-5-1942 First Flight
22-5-1942 9 Maintenance Unit, Cosford
13-7-1942 140 Squadron, Benson
19-7-1942 Flying accident Category.B
         Heston Aircraft Ltd for Merlin 46 Installation
10-11-1942 140 Squadron, Benson (detachments at Mount Farm, St.Eval, Weston Zoyland)
22-5-1945 Struck off charge

BR426   2971
19-5-1942 First Flight
22-5-1942 9 Maintenance Unit, Cosford
6-9-1942   1 Photographic Reconnaissance Unit, Benson (fitted with a W type camera installation)
12-10-1942 47 Maintenance Unit, Sealand
31-10-1942 Benson
6-11-1942 1 Overseas Aircraft Delivery Unit, Portreath
7-11-1942 Ferry flight to Malta
11-11-1942 69 Squadron, Luqa, Malta 'B Flight'
8-12-1942 Shot down by Me109's and aircraft crashed into the sea. Sgt D. T. Howard (k)
Total Flying Hours 111.10

BR427   2977
24-5-1942 First Flight
28-5-1942 1 Photographic Reconnaissance Unit, Benson
27-6-1942 47 Maintenance Unit, Sealand
24-7-1942 'Amot Elkirk' by sea to Takoradi, Gold Coast arrived 11-9-1942
14-9-1942 2 Photographic Reconnaissance Unit, Heliopolis, Egypt
1-2-1943   680 Squadron, Heliopolis, Egypt
1-6-1943   Malta
31-5-1945 Struck off charge

BR428   2976
24-5-1942 First Flight
28-5-1942 1 Photographic Reconnaissance Unit, Benson
6-7-1942   47 Maintenance Unit, Sealand
24-7-1942 'Amot Elkirk' by sea to Takoradi, Gold Coast arrived 11-9-1942
?   2 Photographic Reconnaissance Unit, Heliopolis
1-2-1943   680 Squadron, Heliopolis, Egypt
30-11-1944 Struck off charge

BR429   2978
27-5-1942 First Flight
28-5-1942 1 Photographic Reconnaissance Unit, Benson
27-6-1942 47 Maintenance Unit, Sealand
20-7-1942 'Silver Willow' by sea to Takoradi, Gold Coast arrived 15-8-1942
29-9-1942 2 Photographic Reconnaissance Unit, Heliopolis, Egypt
1-2-1943   680 Squadron, Heliopolis, Egypt
         74 Operational Training Unit, Aqir/Petah Tiqva
10-6-1944 Engine cut out on take-off, Petah Tiqva
31-8-1944 Struck off charge

BR430   2996
30-5-1942   First Flight
31-5-1942   1 Photographic Reconnaissance Unit, Benson
18-6-1942   47 Maintenance Unit, Sealand
21-7-1942   'Wallsend' by sea to Takoradi, Gold Coast arrived 15-8-1942
2-9-1942   2 Photographic Reconnaissance Unit, Heliopolis, Egypt
21-9-1942   Flying accident
1-2-1943   680 Squadron, Heliopolis
14-2-1944   Missing on operations, Crete/Greece

Unidentified Spitfire PR.IV after having a forced-landing on Crete. (Wojtek Matusiak)

BR431   3012
3-6-1942   First Flight
8-6-1942   1 Photographic Reconnaissance Unit, Benson
28-6-1942   9 Maintenance Unit, Cosford
4-8-1942   to Middle East
6-9-1942   69 Squadron, Luqa, Malta 'B Flight'
29-11-1942 3 Photographic Reconnaissance Unit, Pandeveswar, India
13-12-1942 Flying accident
           (681 Squadron, Dum Dum) (aircraft coded 'P')
31-5-1945   Struck off charge

BR432   3005
31-5-1942   First Flight
2-6-1942   1 Photographic Reconnaissance Unit, Benson
27-6-1942   47 Maintenance Unit, Sealand
24-7-1942   'Amot Elkirk' by sea to Takoradi, Gold Coast arrived 11-9-1942
1-10-1942   2 Photographic Reconnaissance Unit, Heliopolis, Egypt
1-2-1943   680 Squadron, Heliopolis
           74 Operational Training Unit, Petah Tiqva, Palestine
25-1-1945   Swung on landing and tipped up onto it's nose, Petah Tiqva

BR433   3020
6-6-1942   First Flight
8-6-1942   1 Photographic Reconnaissance Unit, Benson
27-6-1942   9 Maintenance Unit, Cosford
29-7-1942   Flying accident Category.B to Heston Aircraft Ltd for repair
6-8-1942   Benson
1-3-1943   680 Squadron, Heliopolis, Egypt
20-3-1943   Missing on operations over (Piraeus) Greece

BR434   3033
10-6-1942 First Flight
11-6-1942 1 Photographic Reconnaissance Unit, Benson (fitted with a Y type camera installation)
18-10-1942 Benson
31-10-1942 1 Overseas Aircraft Delivery Unit, Portreath
6-11-1942 4 Photographic Reconnaissance Unit, Gibraltar
13-11-1942 4 Photographic Reconnaissance Unit, Maison Blanche, Algiers, Algeria
20-11-1942 Destroyed in an air raid on Maison Blanche
31-12-142 Struck off charge

BR435   3034
11-6-1942 First Flight
14-6-1942 1 Photographic Reconnaissance Unit, Benson
6-7-1942   47 Maintenance Unit, Sealand
21-7-1942 'Wallsend' by sea to Takoradi, Gold Coast arrived 15-8-1942
2-9-1942   2 Photographic Reconnaissance Unit, Heliopolis, Egypt
23-9-1942 Missing on operations over Crete
14-10-1942 Struck off charge

BR641   3051
14-6-1942 First Flight
21-6-1942 1 Photographic Reconnaissance Unit, Benson
25-7-1942 47 Maintenance Unit, Sealand
29-8-1942 'Nigerstown' by sea to Takoradi, Gold Coast arrived 30-10-1942
2-11-1942 2 Photographic Reconnaissance Unit, Heliopolis, Egypt
1-12-1942 3 Photographic Reconnaissance Unit, Pandeveswar, India
13-12-1942 Struck off charge
Total Flying Hours 55.45

BR642   3052
15-6-1942 First Flight
18-6-1942 1 Photographic Reconnaissance Unit, Benson
14-7-1942 47 Maintenance Unit, Sealand
29-8-1942 'Nigerstown' by sea to Takoradi, Gold Coast arrived 30-10-1942
             128 Squadron, Yundum, Gambia
29-11-1942 Flying accident Category.E

BR643   3061
18-6-1942 First Flight, Engine failed on a test flight and impacted trees during an attempted forced-landing
             and caught fire at Gates House Farm, Lurgashall, near Midhurst Sussex.
             F/O Colin Robert Jarred, a Vickers-Supermarine, Henley production test pilot (k)
8-7-1942   Struck off charge

BR644   3068
20-6-1942 First Flight
26-6-1942 1 Photographic Reconnaissance Unit, Benson
25-7-1942 47 Maintenance Unit, Sealand
29-8-1942 'Nigerstown' by sea to Takoradi, Gold Coast arrived 30-10-1942
1-12-1942 2 Photographic Reconnaissance Unit, Heliopolis, Egypt
1-2-1943   680 Squadron, Heliopolis
26-9-1943 Ran out of and force-landed in Turkey after a PR mission over the Aegean sea. Category.E

BR645   3070
22-6-1942 First Flight
24-6-1942 1 Photographic Reconnaissance Unit, Benson
15-7-1942 47 Maintenance Unit, Sealand
29-8-1942 'Nigerstown' by sea to Takoradi, Gold Coast arrived 30-10-1942
2-11-1942 2 Photographic Reconnaissance Unit, Heliopolis, Egypt
1-2-1943   680 Squadron, Heliopolis
26-9-1943 Returning from a PR mission, crashed near Berka

BR646   3075
22-6-1942 First Flight
23-6-1942 45 Maintenance Unit, Kinloss
3-9-1942   Benson
12-10-1942 47 Maintenance Unit, RAF Sealand
6-11-1942 1 Overseas Aircraft Delivery Unit, Portreath
7-11-1942 Ferry flight to Malta
13-11-1942 2 Photographic Reconnaissance Unit, Heliopolis, Egypt
1-2-1943   680 Squadron, Heliopolis
20-6-1943 Struck off charge, no further details
Total Flying Hours 28.15

BR647   3081
24-6-1942 First Flight
26-6-1942 47 Maintenance Unit, Sealand
7-9-1942   Benson
6-11-1942 1 Overseas Aircraft Delivery Unit, Portreath
7-11-1942 Ferry flight to Malta
13-11-1942 Missing on ferry flight between Gibraltar and Malta

BR648   3082
24-6-1942 First Flight
26-6-1942 45 Maintenance Unit, Kinloss
3-7-1942   140 Squadron, Benson (detachments at Mount Farm, St.Eval, Weston Zoyland)
16-8-1943 on a PR mission the engine failed at 28,000 ft and the aircraft burst into flames and
           was abandoned near Yarcombe, Devon pilot Chuck Sharpe OK

BR649   3101
27-6-1942 First Flight
29-6-1942 45 Maintenance Unit, Kinloss
2-9-1942   Benson
31-10-1942 1 Overseas Aircraft Delivery Unit, Portreath
6-11-1942 4 Photographic Reconnaissance Unit, Gibraltar
13-11-1942 4 Photographic Reconnaissance Unit, Maison Blanche
20-11-1942 Missing on operations, Tunis

BR650   3102
28-6-1942 First Flight
1-7-1942   45 Maintenance Unit, Kinloss
26-8-1942 Benson
10-1942   542 Squadron, Benson (fitted with a W type camera installation)
7-4-1943   Heston Aircraft Ltd
4-1943   543 Squadron, Benson, Mount Farm & St.Eval
11-5-1943 Engine failed and aircraft force-landed 1 mile South-West of Polebrook, Northamptonshire

BR651	3112
2-7-1942	First Flight
3-7-1942	33 Maintenance Unit, Lyneham
15-7-1942	Benson
1-8-1942	8 Operational Training Unit, Dyce
27-8-1942	Flying accident Category.AC
6-3-1943	Failed to return from a high altitude photographic exercise

BR652	3123
4-7-1942	First Flight
8-7-1942	33 Maintenance Unit, Lyneham
9-7-1942	Vickers Armstrong Ltd
15-7-1942	Benson
22-7-1942	8 Operational Training Unit, Dyce
8-9-1942	Flying accident Category.B
6-3-1943	Ferry flight to the Middle East
	680 Squadron, Heliopolis
	74 Operational Training Unit, Aqir/Petah Tiqva
31-5-1945	Struck off charge

BR653	3138
8-7-1942	First Flight
16-7-1942	Benson
11-8-1942	69 Squadron, Luqa, Malta 'B Flight'
1-2-1943	681 Squadron, Dum Dum, Calcutta, India
2-8-1943	Struck off charge

BR654	3139
8-7-1942	First Flight
12-7-1942	39 Maintenance Unit, Colerne
26-7-1942	Benson
13-8-1942	8 Operational Training Unit, RAF Fraserburgh
24-8-1942	Flying accident Category.AC
3-9-1942	Heston Aircraft Ltd for repairs
27-3-1943	Benson
23-4-1943	Ferry flight to Middle East
4-1943	680 Squadron, Heliopolis
	74 Operational Training Unit, Aqir/Petah Tiqva
13-9-1945	Struck off charge

BR655	3140
10-7-1942	First Flight
28-7-1942	Benson
12-7-1942	39 Maintenance Unit, Colerne
28-7-1942	Benson
16-8-1942	8 Operational Training Unit, Fraserburgh
11-9-1942	Flying accident at Montrose Category.E pilot Fred Martyn (k)
17-9-1942	Struck off charge

Total Flying Hours 75.40

BR656   3148
11-7-1942 First Flight
12-7-1942 33 Maintenance Unit, Lyneham
22-12-1942 Benson
12-2-1943 Ferry flight to Malta
2-1943   683 Squadron, Luqa (aircraft coded 'L')
13-4-1943 Hit Spitfire EN146 on landing at Luqa, Malta

BR657   3164
13-7-1942 First Flight
19-7-1942 33 Maintenance Unit, Lyneham
25-7-1942 140 Squadron, Benson (detachments at Mount Farm, St.Eval, Weston Zoyland)
23-4-1943 543 Squadron, Benson, Mount Farm & St.Eval
19-5-1943 1 Overseas Aircraft Delivery Unit, Portreath
17-9-1943 681 Squadron, Dum Dum, Calcutta, India
15-4-1945 Struck off charge

BR658   3165
15-7-1942 First Flight
21-7-1942 ? Maintenance Unit
9-8-1942   1 Photographic Reconnaissance Unit, Benson
19-10-1942 543 Squadron, Benson, Mount Farm & St.Eval
30-6-1943 Flying accident Category.AC
22-10-1943 Benson
3-9-1943   543 Squadron, Vaenga, Northern Russia arrived 4-9 'Operation Source'
1-11-1943 118 ORAP, 118th Independent Reconnaissance Aviation Regiment, Russia
5-12-1943 Struck off charge RAF charge
29-2-1944 Lost in action, (possibly flew into a Mountain in Norway) L I Yelkin (k)
9-12-1944 Struck off Russian charge

BR659   3175
17-7-1942 First Flight
19-7-1942 33 Maintenance Unit, Lyneham
25-7-1942 140 Squadron, Benson (detachments at Mount Farm, St.Eval, Weston Zoyland)
16-8-1943 Benson
18-10-1943 681 Squadron, Dum Dum, Calcutta, India
          74 Operational Training Unit, Petah Tiqva
31-5-1945 Struck off charge

BR660   3178
19-7-1942 First Flight
21-7-1942 33 Maintenance Unit, Lyneham
5-8-1942   1 Photographic Reconnaissance Unit, Benson (fitted with a W type camera installation)
19-10-1942 541 Squadron, Benson
25-1-1943 Abandoned after engine cut out over Guernsey. F/O Allan Greyson Edwards, mssing

BR661   3184
21-7-1942 First Flight
22-7-1942 33 Maintenance Unit, Lyneham
5-8-1942   1 Photographic Reconnaissance Unit, Benson (fitted with a Y type camera installation)
19-10-1942 541 Squadron, Benson
30-4-1943 681 Squadron, Dum Dum, Calcutta, India (aircraft coded 'G')
18-11-1943 Suffered a bird-strike along the coast of Akyab Island but landed safely at Cox's Bazaar.
15-6-1945 Struck off charge

BR662   3189
23-7-1942 First Flight
25-7-1942 1 Photographic Reconnaissance Unit, Benson
12-8-1942 Ferry flight to the Middle East
8-1942   1435 Squadron, Luqa, Malta
18-12-1942 Ditched into sea off Malta. F/Lt Sgt. J. M. Harrison (k)

BR663   3195
24-7-1942 First Flight
25-7-1942 1 Photographic Reconnaissance Unit, Benson
13-8-1942 Ferry flight to Malta
8-1942   69 Squadron, Luqa, Malta 'B Flight'
8-2-1943   680 Squadron, Heliopolis, Egypt
4-4-1943   Failed to return from operations

BR664   3197
25-7-1942 First Flight
25-7-1942 1 Photographic Reconnaissance Unit, Benson
18-10-1942 Benson
31-10-1942 1 Overseas Aircraft Delivery Unit, Portreath
6-11-1942 4 Photographic Reconnaissance Unit, Gibraltar
13-11-1942 4 Photographic Reconnaissance Unit, Maison Blanche
17-12-1942 Flying accident on operations
           680 Squadron, Heliopolis, Egypt
           74 Operational Training Unit, Petah Tiqva
15-3-1944 Undercarriage jammed and aircraft belly-landed, Petah Tiqva
31-5-1944 Struck off charge

BR665   3196
25-7-1942 First Flight
25-7-1942 1 Photographic Reconnaissance Unit, Benson
12-8-1942 Ferry flight to Middle East
8-1942   69 Squadron, Luqa, Malta 'B Flight'
8-2-1943   683 Squadron, Luqa
           Malta Communication Flight
2-8-1945   Struck off charge

BR666   3221
6-8-1942   First Flight
9-8-1942   1 Photographic Reconnaissance Unit, Benson (fitted with a X type camera installation)
26-9-1942 1 Overseas Aircraft Delivery Unit, Portreath
27-9-1942 Ferry flight to Gibraltar
30-10-1942 544 Squadron, Gibraltar 'B Flight'
10-11-1942 Missing on a PR mission to Casablanca, Morocco

BR667   3228
8-8-1942   First Flight
11-8-1942 1 Photographic Reconnaissance Unit, Benson (fitted with a Y type camera installation)
29-8-1947 47 Maintenance Unit, Sealand
8-9-1942   'Ripley' by sea to Takoradi, Gold Coast
27-10-1942 2 Photographic Reconnaissance Unit, Heliopolis, Egypt
           Ferry flight to North-West Africa
1-11-1942 Struck off charge

BR668   3233
9-8-1942   First Flight
10-8-1942   6 Maintenance Unit, Brize Norton
20-9-1942   Benson
3-10-1942   544 Squadron, Gibraltar 'B Flight'
23-12-1942   544 Squadron, detachment to Marrakesh, Morocco
2-11-1943   Heston Aircraft Ltd
15-3-1945   Struck off charge

BR669   3245
12-8-1942   First Flight
13-8-1942   39 Maintenance Unit, Colerne
20-9-1942   Benson
3-10-1942   544 Squadron, Gibraltar 'B Flight'
13-11-1942   Damaged by flak and abandoned 3 miles off Cape Ferrat, France

BR670   3250
14-8-1942   First Flight
15-8-1942   39 Maintenance Unit, Colerne
7-9-1942   RAF Benson
30-9-1942   541 Squadron, Benson (fitted with a Y camera)
3-2-1943   543 Squadron, Benson, Mount Farm & St.Eval
14-3-1943   Engine failed and the aircraft made a wheels-up landing, St.Eval, Cornwall. Category.E

BS355   3267
17-8-1942   First Flight
18-8-1942   6 Maintenance Unit, Brize Norton
31-8-1942   Benson
31-10-1942   1 Overseas Aircraft Delivery Unit, Portreath
6-11-1942   4 Photographic Reconnaissance Unit, Gibraltar
13-11-1942   4 Photographic Reconnaissance Unit, Maison Blanche, Algiers
20-11-1942   Damaged beyond repair during an air raid on Maison Blanche
1-3-1947   Struck off charge

BS356   3290
24-8-1942   First Flight
25-8-1942   6 Maintenance Unit, Brize Norton
30-8-1942   Benson
3-10-1942   1 Overseas Aircraft Delivery Unit, Portreath
6-11-1942   4 Photographic Reconnaissance Unit, Gibraltar
13-11-1942   4 Photographic Reconnaissance Unit, Maison Blanche, Algiers
20-11-1942   Damaged beyond repair during an air raid on Maison Blanche

BS357   3291
24-8-1942   First Flight
26-8-1942   6 Maintenance Unit, Brize Norton
17-9-1942   Benson
9-10-1942   8 Operational Training Unit, Fraserburgh
3-12-1942   Flying accident Category.AC
16-3-1945   Struck off charge

BS358   3292
24-8-1942   First Flight
25-8-1942   6 Maintenance Unit, Brize Norton
31-8-1942   Benson
14-10-1942 47 Maintenance Unit, Sealand
6-11-1942   1 Overseas Aircraft Delivery Unit, Portreath
7-11-1942   Ferry flight to Malta
14-11-1942 Middle East
8-2-1943   683 Squadron, Luqa, Malta
1-5-1943   North West Africa
3-8-1944   Struck off charge (possibly 13-9-1945)

BS359   3302
28-8-1942   First Flight
29-8-1942   6 Maintenance Unit, Brize Norton
8-9-1942   Benson
11-10-1942 47 Maintenance Unit, Sealand
6-11-1942   69 Squadron, Luqa, Malta 'B Flight'
15-11-1942 Failed to return from operations, F/O F. C. M. Jemmett (k)

BS360   3332
4-9-1942   First Flight
7-9-1942   1 Photographic Reconnaissance Unit, Benson (fitted with a Y type camera installation)
9-10-1942   47 Maintenance Unit, Sealand
20-11-1942 'Catrine' by sea to Takoradi, Gold Coast arrived 27-12-1942
            74 Operational Training Unit, Aqir/Petah Tiqva
10-2-1944   Engine caught fire and aircraft abandoned near Petah Tiqva
1-3-1944   Struck off charge

BS361   3405
17-9-1942   First Flight
19-9-1942   1 Photographic Reconnaissance Unit, Benson
10-11-1942 Benson
29-11-1942 1 Overseas Aircraft Delivery Unit, Portreath
1-12-1942   69 Squadron, Malta 'B Flight'
1-2-1943   683 Squadron, Luqa, Malta
28-3-1943   (682 Squadron, Maison Blanche, Algiers, Algeria)
31-10-1943 North African Allied Strategic Command
10-2-1944   Flying accident
31-5-1944   To the French Armee de l'Air GR.II/33, Laghouat
10-6-1944   Destroyed in a ground collision with a Curtiss P-40 at Nettuno. Italy

BS362   3406
17-9-1942   First Flight
19-9-1942   1 Photographic Reconnaissance Unit, Benson, detachment at Leuchars
19-10-1942 540 Squadron, Leuchars
11-10-1942 47 Maintenance Unit, Sealand
20-11-1942 'Catrine' by sea to Takoradi, Gold Coast arrived 27-12-1942
            2 Photographic Reconnaissance Unit, Heliopolis, Egypt
30-4-1943   680 Squadron, Heliopolis
31-10-1943 North African Allied Strategic Command
            74 Operational Training Unit, Petah Tiqva, Israel
29-8-1946   Struck off charge

BS363   3408
19-9-1942   First Flight
22-9-1942   1 Photographic Reconnaissance Unit, Benson
14-10-1942 47 Maintenance Unit, Sealand
20-11-1942 'Catrine' by sea to Takoradi, Gold Coast arrived 27-12-1942
            2 Photographic Reconnaissance Unit, Heliopolis, Egypt
1-2-1943   680 Squadron, Heliopolis
6-12-1945   Struck off charge

BS364   3431
24-9-1942   First Flight
27-9-1942   Benson
31-10-1942 1 Overseas Aircraft Delivery Unit, Portreath
6-11-1942   69 Squadron, Luqa, Malta 'B Flight'
8-2-1943   683 Squadron, Luqa
9-3-1943   Missing on operation to Taranto Naval Base, Naples and Messina, Italy, shot down over Tarranto
            Sgt C. R. Peacock (k)

BS365   3449
30-9-1942   First Flight
1-10-1942   1 Photographic Reconnaissance Unit, Benson
24-10-1942 47 Maintenance Unit, Sealand
20-11-1942 'Catrine' by sea to Takoradi, Gold Coast arrived 27-12-1942
            2 Photographic Reconnaissance Unit, Heliopolis, Egypt
22-1-1943   Engine cut-out and aircraft crash landed in desert 60 miles East-South-East of Beni Suef, Egypt

BS366   3478
10-10-1942 First Flight
12-10-1942 1 Photographic Reconnaissance Unit, Benson
6-11-1942   47 Maintenance Unit, Sealand
30-11-1942 'Tynmouth' by sea to Takoradi, Gold Coast arrived 22-2-1943
16-5-1943   680 Squadron, Heliopolis
            74 Operational Training Unit, Aqir/Petah Tiqva
31-5-1945   Struck off charge

BS367   3492
13-10-1942 First Flight
16-10-1942 1 Photographic Reconnaissance Unit, Benson
6-11-1942   69 Squadron, Luqa, Malta 'B Flight'
10-11-1942 On a PR mission to Taranto, Italy Shot down by ack-ack fire over Augusta, Sicily
            Flt Lt. Harry Coldbeck (PoW)
Total Flying Hours 19.30

BS489   3502
16-10-1942 First Flight
18-10-1942 1 Photographic Reconnaissance Unit, Benson
29-11-1942 1 Overseas Aircraft Delivery Unit, Portreath
1-12-1942   544 Squadron, Gibraltar 'B Flight'
6-12-1942   4 Photographic Reconnaissance Unit, Maison Blanche, Algiers
18-12-1942 Engine cut out and aircraft force-landed Djidjelli, North East Algeria

BS490   3520
17-10-1942 First Flight
21-10-1942 544 Squadron, Benson
29-11-1942 1 Overseas Aircraft Delivery Unit, Portreath
1-12-1942   544 Squadron, Gibraltar 'B Flight'
6-12-1942   4 Photographic Reconnaissance Unit, Maison Blanche, Algiers
12-1942   Flying accident Category.AC
31-12-1942 Struck off charge

BS491   3539
22-10-1942 First Flight
27-10-1942 544 Squadron, Benson
              544 Squadron, Gibraltar 'B Flight'
23-12-1942 544 Squadron, detachment to Marrakesh, Morocco
17-10-1943 541 Squadron, Gibraltar
16-12-1943 Took off at 9.45 am from Gibraltar, and was plotted over the south coast at 2 pm, the aircraft
              ran out of fuel on return to England, F/Lt R. P. Johnson baled out, it is thought that he struck
              the tailplane as his body was found with his parachute unopened a mile from where the aircraft
              crashed at Wraxall, Somerset

BS492   3560
27-10-1942 First Flight
1-11-1942   Benson
6-12-1942   544 Squadron, Gibraltar 'B Flight'
11-8-1943   Heston Aircraft Ltd
22-5-1945   Struck off charge

BS493   3580
31-10-1942 First Flight
2-11-1942   Benson
17-12-1942 47 Maintenance Unit, Sealand
11-1-1943   'Inslanga' by sea to Takoradi, Gold Coast arrived 7-2-1943
2-1943   680 Squadron, Heliopolis
              74 Operational Training Unit, Aqir/Petah Tiqva
13-9-1945   Struck off charge

BS494   3581
31-10-1942 First Flight
2-11-1942   Benson
25-12-1942 4 Photographic Reconnaissance Unit, Gibraltar
28-12-1942 4 Photographic Reconnaissance Unit, Maison Blanche, Algiers
5-1-1943   Suffered damage on operations
1-2-1943   682 Squadron, Maison Blanche
6-2-1943   Collided with Hawker Hurricane HW138 on approach to Maison Blanche

BS495   3594
6-11-1942   First Flight
13-11-1942 Benson
2-12-1942   1 Overseas Aircraft Delivery Unit, Portreath
6-12-1942   Ferry flight to Malta
12-1942   4 Photographic Reconnaissance Unit, Maison Blanche, Algiers
17-12-1942 Missing over Bizerta, Tunisia
31-12-1942 Struck off charge

BS496   3648
21-11-1942 First Flight
29-11-1942 Benson
3-12-1942 1 Overseas Aircraft Delivery Unit, Portreath
7-12-1942 Ferry flight to Malta
12-1942   69 Squadron, Luqa, Malta 'B Flight'
8-2-1943   683 Squadron, Luqa, Malta
2-3-1943   Engine caught fire and aircraft crashed into the sea off Malta enroute to Taranto, Italy possibly flown by Sgt Mickey Tardiff (PoW)

BS500   3683
25-11-1942 First Flight
30-11-1942 Benson
9-12-1942 1 Overseas Aircraft Delivery Unit, Portreath
12-1942   Ferry Flight to Malta via Algiers by John Harold Shelmerdine
12-1942   69 Squadron, Luqa, Malta 'B Flight'
11-1-1943 Missing on a PR mission from Malta

A member of the ground crew handling an F8 camera as the pilot looks on.

Preserved airworthy Reading built
Spitfire PR.XI serial PL965 at Old Warden in August 2009. (DJP)

5 Spitfire PR.XI converted from pre-production Mk.IX fighters
Contract No. B19713/39 Seventh order

These aircraft were constructed as Mk.IX fighters but were converted to PR status
by removing armament and other parts and adding camera installations to the fuselage.
The wing tank alterations were carried out by Supermarine.

BS497   3647
17-11-1942 Weight and centre of gravity loading trials at Worthy Down
21-11-1942 First flight from Worthy Down
23-11-1942 Benson
3-12-1942   542 Squadron, Benson
26-7-1943   543 Squadron, Benson, Mount Farm & St.Eval
23-10-1943 Heston Aircraft Ltd
2-7-1945   8 Operational Training Unit, Haverfordwest
25-7-1946   Dived into ground near Newmarket. Category.E
28-7-1946   Struck off charge

BS498   3682
25-11-1942 First Flight
7-12-1942   Benson
26-3-1943   541 Squadron, Benson (detachment at Leuchars)
13-6-1943   Missing on a PR mission Dortmund Ems Canal, Germany

BS499   3684
29-11-1942 First Flight
7-12-1942   Benson
13-12-1942 541 Squadron, Benson (detachment at Leuchars)
3-4-1943   This aircraft was used to photograph the Möhne dam prior to the Dambusters raid in May,
            flown by F/O J. R. Brew
27-9-1943   Vickers-Armstrongs Supermarine Ltd for Universal Camera Installation
18-6-1944   Benson
27-9-1944   Heston Aircraft Ltd
28-2-1947   to Maintenance Command as 5933M and struck off charge

BS502   3717
6-12-1942   First Flight
7-12-1942   Benson
14-12-1942 542 Squadron, Benson
27-9-1943   Vickers-Armstrongs Supermarine Ltd for Universal Camera Installation
10-1943   Photographic Reconnaissance Development Unit, Benson
11-1943   542 Squadron, Benson
25-2-1944   Failed to return from PR mission to photograph V Rocket sites. F/Sgt H. F. Buckingham (missing)

EN385   3708
2-12-1942   First Flight
9-12-1942   541 Squadron, Benson
7-2-1943   Failed to return from a PR mission to Cologne and Duisburg, Germany
            F/O John Clifford Taffs (missing)

According to Gordon Painters notebook that he kept he worked on six Mk.XI Spitfires at Henley,
the missing one could possibly have been BS501 which is listed as being built/assembled at Benson.

2 x Spitfire Vb fighters built against contract No. B19713/39 Fourth order

AA933   2257
31-10-1941 First Flight
7-11-1941   6 Maintenance Unit, Brize Norton
22-11-1941 145 Squadron, Catterick, Yorkshire
1-2-1942   Flying accident Category.B
10-2-1942   350 Squadron, Valley (aircraft coded 'MN-B')
26-9-1942   234 Squadron, Portreath
10-12-1942 303 Squadron, Kirton-in-Lindsey, Lincolnshire
29-3-1943   Flying accident Category.AC
31-8-1943   504 Squadron, Redhill, Surrey
22-9-1943   313 Squadron, Ibsley, Hampshire
25-2-1944   144 Affiliation Flight
27-3-1944   442 Squadron, Holmsley South, Hampshire
28-3-1944   Vickers-Armstrongs Ltd
5-1944   2 Tactical Exercise Unit, Grangemouth, Falkirk
25-6-1944   61 Operational Training Unit, Rednal, Shropshire
18-11-1944 Dived into ground whilst coming out of clouds near Wrexham

AA934   2258
31-10-1941 First Flight
7-11-1941   6 Maintenance Unit, Brize Norton
22-11-1941 145 Squadron, Catterick
11-2-1942   350 Squadron, Valley, Anglesey (aircraft coded 'MN-J')
19-2-1942   350 Squadron, Atcham, Shropshire
30-4-1942   Damaged by flak on a Roadstead operation near Calais, France. Category.E
           Struck off charge

2 x Spitfire Vc fighters built against contract No. B19713/39 Fourth order

AB461   2591
14-2-1942   First Flight
17-2-1942   8 Maintenance Unit, Little Rissington
8-3-1942   66 Squadron, Portreath
30-7-1942   On convoy patrol, aircraft spun into the sea 5 miles off St.Albans Head, Dorset. Sgt J. Beasley (k)

AB462   2592
14-2-1942   First Flight
17-2-1942   8 Maintenance Unit, Little Rissington
8-3-1942   66 Squadron, Portreath (aircraft coded 'LZ-W')
24-3-1942   Collided with Spitfire AB496 during a night flight, crashed Frithen Farm, 1½ miles SW
           of St.Erth, Cornwall
4-4-1942   Air Service Training Ltd, Hamble
6-5-1942   Struck off charge

27 x Spitfire Vc fighters built against contract No. B19713/39 Fifth order

BP957   2671
13-3-1942   First Flight
23-3-1942   6 Maintenance Unit, Brize Norton
28-3-1942   47 Maintenance Unit, Sealand
31-3-1942   'SS Empire Heath' by sea to Takoradi, Ghana
8-6-1942   603 Squadron, Ta Qali
9-7-1942   Shot down into sea off Malta. F/O G. A. Levy-Despas (k)
10-7-1942   Struck off charge

BP960   2647
7-3-1942   First Flight
12-3-1942 6 Maintenance Unit, Brize Norton
23-3-1942 82 Maintenance Unit, Lichfield, Staffordshire
31-3-1942 'SS Empire Heath' by sea to Takoradi, Gold Coast
           Malta
10-5-1942 Shot down into sea off Malta. Category.E
12-5-1942 Struck off charge

Spitfire Vc(T) BR226 being loaded onto the USS Wasp at King George V dock at Glasgow. note extra fuel drop tank under the fuselage and Vokes tropical filter below the engine. (Wojtek Matusiak)

BR226   2710
23-3-1942 First Flight
29-3-1942 39 Maintenance Unit, Colerne
12-4-1942 Delivered to Renfrew, Glasgow
1-5-1942   Loaded onto carrier 'USS Wasp' from King George V dock at Glasgow 'Operation Bowery'
9-5-1942   flew off carrier to Malta
18-5-1943 Flying accident Category.B
1-6-1943   126 Squadron, Safi
1-11-1943 249 Squadron, Ta Qali
4-5-1945   Shot down by Bf.109 near Naxxar
26-5-1945 Struck off charge
21-6-1945 Brought back on charge
30-8-1945 Struck off charge

BR227   2735
27-3-1942 First Flight
29-3-1942 ? Maintenance Unit
11-4-1942 Delivered to Renfrew, Glasgow
12-4-1942 Loaded onto carrier 'USS Wasp' from King George V dock at Glasgow 'Operation Calendar'
20-4-1942 flew off carrier to Malta
7-1942   249 Squadron, Ta Qali, Malta (aircraft coded 'T-T')
8-7-1942   Shot down Malta, P/O J. C. Gilbert (k)
9-7-1942   Struck off charge

BR228   2761
1-4-1942   First Flight
3-4-1942   37 Maintenance Unit, Burtonwood, Staffordshire
18-4-1942 47 Maintenance Unit, Sealand
9-5-1942   India
1-8-1942   Middle East
30-11-1943 218 Group, North Africa
8-3-1944   Struck off charge

BR229   2811
12-4-1942   First Flight
14-4-1942   39 Maintenance Unit, Colerne
28-4-1942   Ferried Colerne to Prestwick by Lettice Curtis t/o 19.00 landed 20.45
29-4-1942   Delivered to Renfrew, Glasgow
1-5-1942   Loaded onto carrier 'USS Wasp' from King George V dock at Glasgow 'Operation Bowery'
9-5-1942   flew off carrier to Malta
5-1942   Malta
            Struck off charge

BR230   2793
10-4-1942   First Flight
18-4-1942   39 Maintenance Unit, Colerne
29-4-1942   Delivered to Renfrew
10-5-1942   'SS Empire Conrad' by sea to Gibraltar 'Operation Style or Salient' 6-1942
            Flown to Malta off carrier 'HMS Eagle'
6-1942   185 Squadron, Malta
16-6-1942   Shot down by Bf.109s off Malta. Category.E
18-6-1942   Struck off charge

BR231   2870
27-4-1942   First Flight
29-4-1942   39 Maintenance Unit, Colerne
3-5-1942   Vickers-Armstrongs Ltd for fitting of Tropical Filter
6-5-1942   47 Maintenance Unit, Sealand
10-5-1942   'SS Empire Conrad' by sea to Gibraltar 'Operation Style or Salient' 6-1942
            Flown to Malta off carrier 'HMS Eagle'
6-1942   603 Squadron, Ta Qali
8-6-1942   Shot down over Malta. F/O Leslie G. Barlow (k)
9-6-1942   Struck off charge

BR232   2873
30-4-1942   First Flight
30-4-1942   39 Maintenance Unit, Colerne
3-5-1942   Vickers-Armstrongs Ltd for fitting of Tropical Filter
6-5-1942   47 Maintenance Unit, Sealand
10-5-1942   'SS Empire Conrad' by sea to Gibraltar 'Operation Style or Salient' 6-1942
            Flown to Malta off carrier 'HMS Eagle'
1-7-1942   Middle East
7-1942   601 Squadron, Mariut
6-7-1942   Failed to return from operations, presumed shot down by Bf.109's near El Daba, Egypt

BR233   2912
6-5-1942   First Flight
7-5-1942   39 Maintenance Unit, Colerne
16-5-1942   47 Maintenance Unit, Sealand
26-5-1942   'SS Hopetarn' by sea to Gibraltar 'Operation Style or Salient' 6-1942
            Flown to Malta off carrier 'HMS Eagle'
4-7-1942   249 Squadron, Ta Qali (aircraft coded 'T-Q')
8-7-1942   Shot down in sea off Malta, F/O J. Smith (k)
9-7-1942   Struck off charge
Total Flying Hours 25.05

BR234   2979
27-5-1942   First Flight
28-5-1942   39 Maintenance Unit, Colerne
10-6-1942   82 Maintenance Unit, Lichfield
20-6-1942   'SS Nigerstown' by sea to Takoradi, Gold Coast
1-8-1942   Middle East possibly with 123 Squadron
            Converted by 103 Maintenance Unit, Aboukir, Egypt as high altitude fighter
13-9-1942   Struck off charge

BR235   3006
31-5-1942   First Flight
2-6-1942   8 Maintenance Unit, Little Rissington
18-6-1942   47 Maintenance Unit, Sealand
20-6-1942   'SS Nigerstown' by sea to Takoradi, Gold Coast
22-7-1942   Middle East
8-1942   92 Squadron, North Africa
9-1942   145 Squadron, North Africa
6-9-1942   Flying accident
30-11-1943 218 Group North Africa
18-4-1944   Engine cut and the undercarriage collapsed on landing, Petah Tiqva
29-6-1944   Struck off charge

BR236   3024
5-6-1942   First Flight
8-6-1942   8 Maintenance Unit, Little Rissington
8-7-1942   55 Maintenance Unit, Holywood, Dumfries & Galloway
19-7-1942   'SS Empire Clive' by sea to Gibraltar 'Operation Bellows or Baritone' 8-1942
            Flown to Malta off carrier 'HMS Furious'
            1435 Squadron, Luqa
25-11-1942 Missing on operations
27-11-1942 Struck off charge
Total Flying Hours 79.50

Spitfire Vc/Tropical delivered to Australia

BR237   3038
13-6-1942   First Flight
22-6-1942   8 Maintenance Unit, Little Rissington
19-7-1942   215 Maintenance Unit, Tinwald Downs, Dumfries & Galloway
4-8-1942   'SS Hoperidge' by sea to Australia arrived Melbourne 23-10-1942
30-10-1942 1 Air Depot, Laverton, Victoria
26-11-1942 452 Squadron, Mascot, New South Wales as A58-15
6-2-1943   Engine failed during combat, aircraft hit power lines nr Strauss airstrip, aircraft abandoned

BR238 after a forced-landing.
(Peter Malone Collection)

BR238   3069
21-6-1942   First Flight
26-6-1942   6 Maintenance Unit, Brize Norton
19-7-1942   215 Maintenance Unit, Tinwald Downs
4-8-1942   'SS Hoperidge' by sea to Australia arrived Melbourne 23-10-1942
4-11-1942   1 Air Depot, Laverton, Victoria
6-12-1942   2 Operational Training Unit, Mildura, Victoria to A58-16
15-12-1943 Damaged on landing Mildura
15-2-1943   Wheels-up landing 4 miles east of Yatpool
8-3-1943   2 Air Depot, Richmond, New South Wales
14-7-1943   457 Squadron, Livingstone, Northern Territory
12-2-1944   Crashed on landing Drysdale
15-3-1944   7 Repair and Salvage Unit, Darwen
27-3-1944   457 Squadron, Livingstone
21-4-1944   7 Repair and Salvage Unit, Darwen
7-5-1944   457 Squadron, Livingstone
16-7-1944   6 Air Depot, Oakey, Queensland
5-1-1945   85 Squadron, (aircraft coded 'SH-R')
29-6-1945   Wheels-up landing Pearce
3-7-1945   17 Repair and Salvage Unit
23-7-1945   85 Squadron, Pearce, Western Australia
10-10-1945 6 Air Depot, Oakey, Queensland
22-3-1946   Category.E storage
22-5-1946   Struck off charge
26-11-1947 DAP
15-11-1948 Struck off charge

BR239   3080
24-6-1942   First Flight
26-6-1942   6 Maintenance Unit, Brize Norton
16-7-1942   47 Maintenance Unit, Sealand
30-7-1942   'SS Eurybates' by sea to Australia arrived Melbourne 18-10-1942
19-10-1942 1 Air Depot, Laverton, Victoria
11-11-1942 54 Squadron, Richmond, New South Wales as A58-17
2-5-1943   Shot down and abandoned with the aircraft crashing into the sea 20 Miles
             south-west of Perin Is. F/O G. C. Farries rescued

BR240 as A58-18 'SH-Y serving with 85 Squadron, in company
with other Spitfires. (Peter Malone Collection)

BR240   3109
30-6-1942   First Flight
1-7-1942   6 Maintenance Unit, Brize Norton
24-7-1942   215 Maintenance Unit, Tinwald Downs
4-8-1942   'SS Hoperidge' by sea to Australia arrived Melbourne 23-10-1942
4-11-1942   1 Air Depot, Laverton, Victoria
28-11-1942 452 Squadron, Mascot, New South Wales as A58-18 (aircraft coded 'QY-Y')
23-7-1943   Undercarriage selector lever jammed and landed wheels-up Pell Field flown by P/O D. Evans
25-7-1943   7 Repair and Salvage Unit, Darwen
9-8-1943   452 squadron, Strauss, Northern Territory
13-2-1944   14 Aircraft Repair Depot
9-3-1944   54 Squadron, Winnellie, Northern Territory
17-3-1944   7 Repair and Salvage Unit, Darwen
1-4-1944   457 Squadron, Livingstone, Northern Territory
16-7-1944   6 Air Depot, Oakey, Queensland
6-12-1944   85 Squadron, (aircraft coded 'SH-Y')
8-10-1945   4 Air Depot
11-2-1946   6 Air Depot, Oakey, Queensland
22-3-1946   Category.E Storage
30-4-1946   CRD Converted to components

BR241 as A58-19 after a forced-landing. (Peter Malone Collection)

BR241   3111
1-7-1942   First Flight
4-7-1942   6 Maintenance Unit, Brize Norton
25-7-1942   215 Maintenance Unit, Tinwald Downs
4-8-1942   'SS Hoperidge' by sea to Australia arrived Melbourne 23-10-1942
            via the Commonwealth Aircraft Corporation
28-10-1942 1 Air Depot, Laverton, Victoria
9-11-1942   452 Squadron, Mascot, New South Wales as A58-19 (aircraft coded 'QY-T')
23-1-1943   Wheels-up landing Batchelor
14-2-1943   7 Repair and Salvage Unit, Darwen
18-2-1943   452 Squadron, Strauss, Northern Territory
2-5-1943   Hit in combat and force-landed
30-6-1943   Engine cut-out during interception and crash landed Strauss airstrip flown by P/O J. Lamberton
21-7-1943   Converted to components

BS218   3147
12-7-1942 8 Maintenance Unit, Little Rissington
25-7-1942 47 Maintenance Unit, Sealand
4-8-1942   'SS Hoperidge' by sea to Australia arrived Melbourne 23-10-1942
30-10-1942 1 Air Depot, Laverton, Victoria
10-11-1942 1 Fighter Wing to A58-83
29-11-1942 Engine overheated and aircraft force-landed Norellan NSW
7-12-1942 2 Air Depot, Richmond, New South Wales
3-2-1943   7 Air Depot
13-5-1943 54 Squadron, Winnellie, Northern Territory
12-10-1943 Crashed during night landing, Darwin
16-10-1943 7 Repair and Salvage Unit, Darwen
9-1-1944   457 Squadron, Livingstone, Northern Territory
16-6-1944 9 Repair and Salvage Unit
7-8-1944   14 Aircraft Repair Depot Replenishment Pool
24-9-1944 85 Squadron, Guildford, Western Australia
10-10-1945 6 Air Depot, Oakey, Queensland
22-3-1946 Category.E Storage
26-11-1947 DAP
15-11-1948 Struck off charge

BS219 as A58-84 with 'Jiminy Cricket' cartoon character artwork in front of the cockpit when flown by F/O Hamilton. (Peter Malone Collection)

BS219   3176
18-7-1942 First Flight
19-7-1942 8 Maintenance Unit, Little Rissington
20-7-1942 47 Maintenance Unit, Sealand
4-8-1942   'SS Hoperidge' by sea to Australia arrived Melbourne 23-10-1942
28-10-1942 1 Air Depot, Laverton, Victoria
9-11-1942 1 Fighter Wing to A58-84
9-11-1942 457 Squadron, Camden, New South Wales (aircraft coded 'ZP-X' 'Jiminy Cricket')
12-10-1943 Undershot on landing Livingstone
13-10-1943 7 Repair and Salvage Unit, Darwen
14-12-1943 452 Squadron, Strauss, Northern Territory
16-6-1944 14 Aircraft Repair Depot Replenishment Pool
21-6-1944 14 Aircraft Repair Depot
22-9-1944 2 Operational Training Unit, Mildura, Victoria
1-11-1944 8 Operational Training Unit, Parkes, New South Wales, suffered a take-off accident 11-1944
27-3-1945 6 Air Depot, Oakey, Queensland
9-8-1945   CRD Converted to components

BS220   3246
12-8-1942   First Flight
13-8-1942   6 Maintenance Unit, Brize Norton
20-8-1942   47 Maintenance Unit, Sealand
9-9-1942   'SS Port Sydney' by sea to Australia arrived Melbourne 29-11-1942
29-11-1942 2 Air Depot, Richmond, New South Wales
8-12-1942   54 Squadron, Richmond, New South Wales to A58-85 (aircraft coded 'DL-Z')
2-5-1943   Crashed landed at end of runway due to fuel shortage in combat,
3-5-1943   7 Repair and Salvage Unit, Darwen
12-7-1943   54 Squadron, Winnellie, Northern Territory
9-4-1944   452 Squadron, Strauss, Northern Territory
29-5-1944   Crashed landed due to brake failure, Darwin
31-5-1944   9 Repair and Salvage Unit
13-7-1944   14 Aircraft Repair Depot Replenishment Pool
27-7-1944   14 Aircraft Repair Depot
29-9-1944   4 Aircraft Repair Depot Replenishment Pool
3-10-1944   4 Aircraft Repair Depot
18-10-1944 85 Squadron, Livingstone, Northern Territory
10-9-1945   17 Repair and Salvage Unit
7-11-1945   CRD Converted to components

BS221   3249
14-8-1942   First Flight
15-8-1942   8 Maintenance Unit, Little Rissington
22-8-1942   215 Maintenance Unit, Tinwald Downs
29-8-1942   'SS Raranga' by sea to Australia arrived Melbourne 10-11-1942
10-11-1942 1 Air Depot, Laverton, Victoria
27-11-1942 54 Squadron, Richmond, New South Wales to A58-86 (aircraft coded 'DL-N')
2-5-1943   Engine failed, aircraft suffering a glycol leak and abandoned over Darwin

BS222   3297
24-8-1942   First Flight
26-8-1942   6 Maintenance Unit, Brize Norton
10-9-1942   215 Maintenance Unit, Tinwald Downs
9-10-1942   'SS Port Wyndham' by sea to Australia arrived Melbourne 21-11-1942
25-11-1942 1 Air Depot, Laverton, Victoria
17-12-1942 2 Operational Training Unit, Mildura, Victoria as A58-87
19-1-1943   Flew into water during gunnery practice, Lake Victoria North-East of Adelaide NSW
            Sgt Herbert Thomas Tanser (k)

BS223   3311
30-8-1942   First Flight
1-9-1942   39 Maintenance Unit, Colerne
26-9-1942   215 Maintenance Unit, Tinwald Downs
9-10-1942   'SS Port Wyndham' by sea to Australia arrived Melbourne 21-11-1942
25-11-1942 1 Air Depot, Laverton, Victoria
28-2-1943   No.2 Fighter Sector as A58-14
26-3-1943   2 Operational Training Unit, Mildura, Victoria
9-5-1943   1 Fighter Wing
14-5-1943   452 Squadron, Strauss, Northern Territory
20-9-1943   14 Aircraft Repair Depot
24-9-1943   452 Squadron, Strauss, Northern Territory
24-4-1944   7 Repair and Salvage Unit
7-5-1944   452 Squadron, Strauss, Northern Territory
15-6-1944   14 Aircraft Repair Depot Replenishment Pool
17-8-1944   2 Operational Training Unit, Mildura, Victoria
23-8-1945   CRD Converted to components

BS224 with 2 OTU, Mildura 1944.
(Peter Malone Collection)

BS224	3317
31-8-1942	First Flight
1-9-1942	39 Maintenance Unit, Colerne
26-9-1942	215 Maintenance Unit, Tinwald Downs
9-10-1942	'SS Port Wyndham' by sea to Australia arrived Melbourne 21-11-1942
24-11-1942	1 Air Depot, Laverton, Victoria
6-12-1942	2 Operational Training Unit, Mildura, Victoria (aircraft coded '4') later A58-88
27-2-1943	24 Squadron?
25-3-1943	Ground-looped on landing, Williamstown
10-4-1943	2 Air Depot, Richmond, New South Wales
13-6-1944	2 Operational Training Unit, Mildura, Victoria
22-6-1944	Engine failed and aircraft force-landed, Mildura
1-11-1944	8 Operational Training Unit, Parkes, New South Wales
14-11-1945	6 Air Depot, Oakey, Queensland
22-3-1946	Category.E to storage
26-11-1947	DAP
15-11-1948	Struck off charge

BS225 which later became A58-89.
(Peter Malone Collection)

BS225	3322
31-8-1942	First Flight
1-9-1942	39 Maintenance Unit, Colerne
23-9-1942	215 Maintenance Unit, Tinwald Downs
13-10-1942	'SS Waroonga' by sea to Australia arrived Melbourne 24-12-1942
25-12-1942	1 Air Depot, Laverton, Victoria
17-2-1943	7 Air Depot
	2 Operational Training Unit, Mildura, Victoria A58-89 (aircraft coded '5')
31-3-1943	452 Squadron, Strauss, New Territory (aircraft coded 'QY-B')
2-5-1943	Shot down by a Mitsubishi Zero during an air-raid on Darwin Harbour

BS226   3333
5-9-1942   First Flight
7-9-1942   6 Maintenance Unit, Brize Norton
13-9-1942 215 Maintenance Unit, Tinwald Downs
9-10-1942 'SS Port Wyndham' by sea to Australia arrived Melbourne 21-11-1942
27-11-1942 1 Air Depot, Laverton, Victoria
19-1-1943 7 Air Depot
24-2-1943 457 Squadron, Livingstone, New Territory as A58-90
8-3-1943   7 Repair and Salvage Unit, Darwen
13-3-1943 452 Squadron, Strauss, Northern Territory (aircraft coded 'QY-A')
2-5-1943   Ran out of fuel after combat interception crashed landed in shallows off Tumbling Waters NT
10-5-1943 7 Repair and Salvage Unit, Darwen
23-5-1943 14 Aircraft Repair Depot

1 x Spitfire F.IXc built against contract No. B19713/39 Seventh order

EN286   3715
4-12-1942 First Flight
6-12-1942 6 Maintenance Unit, Brize Norton
20-12-1942 47 Maintenance Unit, Sealand
10-1-1943 'SS Skeldergate' by sea to Gibraltar
6-2-1943   Gibraltar
31-3-1943 North West Africa
1-7-1943   1 Squadron, South African Air Force, Pachino, Sicily (coded 'AX-8' named 'Cire Cooks VIII')
19-7-1943 Destroyed a Bf.109 near Randazzo, Sicily
13-8-1943 Ran out of fuel on operation and force-landed, Lentini West. Category.FB/B repaired in works
30-11-1943 North Africa
12-5-1945 2 Squadron, South African Air Force, Ravenna, Italy
2-8-1945   Middle East
27-2-1947 to the Royal Hellenic Air Force

Two other Spitfires are listed as being with Vickers-Armstrongs at Henley these are both Mk.IX aircraft, MK694 noted as being with Vickers-Armstrongs 30-8-1945 and RK889 which was a presentation aircraft 'Edmonton II' this had a minor accident serving with 313 Squadron and is noted as repaired on site possibly by Vickers. Both of these aircraft ended up serving with the Danish Air Force. These dates do not tie in with Spitfire production here which finished at the end of 1942.

Spitfire HF.IXe 41-420 ex RK889.
Royal Danish AF at Værløse AFB in 1953
serving with No.722 Squadron.
(RDAF-photo, SnSg. Birger Mikkelsen)

Operations Orator, Source and Tungsten

Brief explanations of operations involving Henley built Spitfire PR.IV's

Orator

This involved a detachment of three Spitfire PR.IV's (BP889, BP891, and BP923) from 1 Photographic Reconnaissance Unit, Benson which flew out to Vaenga, near Murmansk from Sumburgh on Shetland on the 1st September 1942. They flew via the airfield at Afrikanda and arrived at Vaenga on the 2nd September. This was to protect Convey PQ18 which was to sail for Russia on the 3rd. On the 9th September one of the aircraft (BP891) was damaged during a German bombing raid and was later to be used to provide spares and was replaced on the 19th September when a spare aircraft AB132 was flown out. On the 27th the unit suffered its first casualty when BP889 was shot down during a low-level mission to Atlenfjord. The last mission was flown on 15th October and on the 18th October the surviving aircraft AB132, BP923 plus the spares donor BP891 were handed over to the Soviets.
(Spitfires BP889 and BP891 were built at High Post Aerodrome)

Source

The 3rd September 1943 brought another detachment to Vaenga with another three Spitfires (AB423, AB427 and BR658) of 543 Squadron, Benson. Again they left from Sumburgh flying direct and arrived the day after on the 4th. Operation 'Source' was to involve the photographing of the warships Tirpitz and Scharnhorst, on the 22nd September the Tirpitz was damaged by midget submarines. The detachment carried out 31 missions altogether 25 of which were successful. The crew handing over the their aircraft to the Soviets on the 31st October.

Unidentified Russian Spitfire missing from a recce mission over Altafjord 3rd November 1943 flown by Lieutenant Belyakov could be either AB423 or AB427

Tungsten

The final detachment to Russia involved four Spitfires (BP884, BP917, BP926 and BP929) of 542 Squadron, although only three left on the 7th March 1944 one staying behind. They flew the same route as the previous operations from Sumburgh flying directly to Vaenga. One of the aircraft was damaged by flak on the 10th March*. Operation Tungsten again involved photographing the Tirpitz and on the 3rd April the ship was attacked although due to bad weather photo's could not be obtained until the 7th. The spare aircraft eventually had to be flown out on the 19th April* although this did not make it as it force-landed on the way. The detachment left for home on the 31st May again leaving all the serviceable aircraft for the Soviets.

Unidentified Russian Spitfire shot down during a recce to Kirkenes, Norway 16th May 1944 flown by Captain Viktor V Aleksandrov could be either AB423 or AB427

The following are individual aircraft handed over to the Russians whose identity cannot be confirmed but could be from either BP884, BP917, BP929.

*One unidentified aircraft flown by S/L Furniss RAF damaged by Russian ground fire resulting in a forced-landing at Afrikanda airfield on the c.10th March 1944.

*One unidentified spare aircraft flown by F/O Gorrill RAF force-landed due to mechanical failure on the 19th April 1944

Unidentified Spitfire marked '02' marked as "Meibl" flown by captain Iosif A Platonov force-landed at Pumanki on the 29th June 1944 and was later transferred in 1946 to the Northern Fleet Museum, Murmansk although this has never been confirmed.

Spitfire BP926 shot down during recce over Kirkenes, Norway 18th June 1944
Senior Lieutenant I. J. Popovich baled out, The aircraft remains have recently been recovered.

Johnnie Wakefield

John Peter Wakefield, pictured above with his wife Kay whom he married in 1938 was born in Marylebone, London on 5th April 1915. The son of explosives manufacturer W. H. Wakefield, he started racing motorcycles as well as being an accomplished skier and later he established himself as a car racing driver during the 1930's, and entered many races of which he won the Grand Prix of Naples in 1939 driving a Maserati. He bought himself a BA Eagle aircraft G-AEER in 1936 which he flew to various locations when he was motor racing until he sold it in October 1937. He joined the Fleet Air Arm in late 1940 with the rank of Lieutenant, but resigned with effect from the 25th March 1942. He became a test pilot for Vickers-Supermarine and resided in Hamble, Hampshire at the Bugle Hotel. It was while he was due to test fly Spitfire IV BR413 from Henley on the 24th April 1942 that he had to take avoiding action during take-off when a Miles Magister training aircraft belonging to 8 Elementary Flying Training School strayed into his path, there was no traffic control at the airfield. The aircraft took off, swung and he lost control and it crashed and then caught fire. He is buried in a family grave at Seddon near Symonds Yat overlooking the Wye Valley, although his memory lives on as The Johnny Wakefield Trophy is awarded to the driver setting the fastest race lap of the season in Formula 1. (With thanks to John MacMillan for the information and pictures)

Johnnie Wakefield being congratulated by Princess Birabongse of Siam after winning the J.C.C. 200 mile race at Brooklands in his ERA 1500cc supercharged racing car in 1938.

529 (ROTA) SQUADRON

Avro Rota I DR624 'KX-L' of 529 (Rota) Squadron (RTR Collection)

Arriving at Henley between the 16th and 18th of August 1944 was 529 (Rota) Squadron from it's then base of Halton in Buckinghamshire, this move was because of the threat of German rocket attacks on London, Halton had been chosen as a possible relocation site for certain government offices, on 23rd August 1944, at a conference at HQ Technical Training Command, orders were given to evacuate all trainees and staff to RAF Cosford, Shropshire and Locking, Avon on the 28th August. This order was carried out by the 5th September and Halton was put under Care & Maintenance. By the end of September the planned move had been cancelled.

Henley now became a proper RAF station with the arrival of the Squadron, and now had both based aircraft and personnel permanently on site for the first time. The Squadron had been formed from No.1448 Radar Calibration Flight on the 15th June 1943. The main duties of the Squadron being the calibration of the various radar stations, and radar defence equipment for anti-aircraft guns that were situated around the country, using the Avro Rota Autogiro and de Havilland Hornet Moth, 529 Squadron was the only RAF Squadron to use the Autogiro. During December 1939 it was decided that the coastal radar defences needed to be refined and Autogiros were felt to be ideally suited to the type of calibration work required. It fell to the Cierva Autogiro Company to resolve the issue and in early 1940 Mr R. Brie of the company successfully completed tests using four autogiros.

The Autogiro had played an important part in the Battle of Britain for without it the radar that detected the incoming enemy attacks would probably not have been quite so effective and it is because of the very secretive nature of this work that very little was known at the time exactly what they were used for. The Autogiros were operated on detachment, and were usually based at the nearest airfield to the radar station, normally the pilot would be accompanied by an engine fitter and rigger. They were used for calibrating the east and south coast Chain Home (CH) radar stations, these formed a link of stations from Scotland down to and along the south coast of England.

The calibration of a radar station was not a lengthy task, but sometimes took longer depending on how favourable the weather conditions were. When a station was due for a calibration check one or two members of 60 Group were sent to the site and would first make sure that the station was operational.

For the actual calibration the Autogiro would fly in a tight a circle as possible known as orbiting at a selected point at varying different ranges, heights and bearings allowing accurate radar readings to be taken, these were known as azimuth calibrations. The Autogiro was fitted with a transponder situated in the forward cockpit which the receiving radar aerial could then pick-up a signal from, the measured bearings taken could then be averaged and then compared with a final known bearing. Using charts that had been drawn up by a team at 60 Group headquarters these readings could be used to ascertain the angles of elevation taken from the known heights and range and these then provided the data for the stations Electrical Calculator computer operated by the crew on the ground.

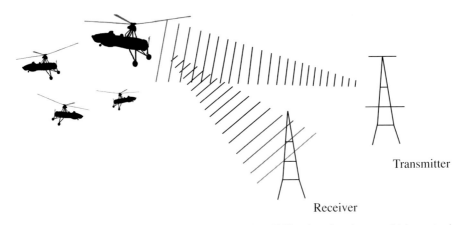

Transmitter

Receiver

An example of a Chain Home Radar Station Calibration showing an orbiting autogiro

Other work undertaken by the Autogiros during 1944 was in accordance with the establishment of Anti-Aircraft (AA) sites on the east coast because of the threat from V1 rocket attacks.

The Autogiros always had a fighter escort either provided by the Royal Air Force or Fleet Air Arm depending in which areas they were operating, and there were a few instances where German fighters appeared, one occasion being in July 1943 when F/Lt Hill was attacked by two Focke-Wulf 190s, several others did come under fire but their agility and the rapid intervention of the escorting fighters usually saved them, and no Autogiro was ever lost in action.

A de Havilland Hornet Moth, this particular example is in 502 Squadron markings and is seen at a fly-in at Kemble, Gloucestershire in May 2010, the Hornet Moths of 529 Squadron went to 5 MU at Kemble for disposal and onward sale. (DJP)

De Havilland Hornet Moths were also used for calibration of radar and anti-aircraft guns and were fitted with a device called a Squegging Oscillator, an electronic circuit which produces a radio-frequency output in short bursts which was tuned to the frequency of the radar station. The aircraft would be flown directly overhead on set height designated bearings and tracked until no longer visible, the pilot would then call-in via the radio and would be requested to return on a reciprocal bearing, whilst again being tracked, as the aircraft returned into view a reading could then be obtained. These readings produced what were known as a vertical polar diagram which would show the radar operators the areas where aircraft could be detected. Ten Hornet Moths were on strength with the Squadron during it's time at Henley and were kept fairly busy with calibration work.

Aircraft used by 529 (Rota) Squadron at Henley-on-Thames
The Aircraft were allocated the code letters of KX-

Avro 671 Rota 1 Autogiro (Cierva C30A)
K4232
K4233 'KX-F'
K4235 'KX-B' or 'KX-H'
K4239 'KX-J'
Impressed into service with the RAF from civilian use.

V1187 'KX-O'	ex G-ACWO
AP506 'KX-A'	ex G-ACWM
AP507 'KX-H'	ex G-ACWP
AP509 'KX-E'?	ex G-ACWS
AP510 'KX-E'?	ex G-ACYE
BV999	ex G-ACXW
DR622 'KX-X'	ex G-ACYH
DR623 'KX-N'	ex G-ACWH
DR624 'KX-L'	ex G-ACWF
HM580 'KX-K'	ex G-ACUU
HM581	ex G-ACUI

de Havilland Hornet Moth

Hornet Moths were impressed into service with the RAF from civilian use.

W5749	ex G-ADKK
W5750 'KX-Y'	ex G-ADKL
W5754 'KX-W'	ex G-ADKW
W5777	ex G-AEWY
W5779 'KX-S'	ex G-AFDT
W5830	ex G-ADKE
W9383	ex G-AEKY
W9389	ex G-ADMJ
X9310	ex G-ADMR
AV952 'KX-T'	ex G-ADSK

Airspeed Oxford I & II

used for Communications & Transport
T1210
X7238

de Havilland Tiger Moth II

T6864

Airspeed Oxford I. (DJP)

THE FIRST HELICOPTERS

The first unit in the RAF to use the Sikorsky Hoverfly helicopter, was the Helicopter Training Flight at Andover, Hampshire. Formed in February 1945, and initially referred to as 'D' Flight.

Pilots of existing Army Air Observation Posts (AOP) and 529 Squadron were to be converted to the Helicopters, and during the month S/L Basil Arkell was drafted in as the Flights Commanding Officer, he and F/Lt J. F. Cable had been on a conversion course at the USCG station at Floyd Bennett Field in New York. Eventually four instructors, including F/Lts R. Bradbury, Jimmy Harper and George Ford from 529 Squadron joined the unit after they to had received training at Andover.

During March 1945 the Helicopter Training Flight was merged as a separate unit into a part of 43 Operational Training Unit (OTU) also based at Andover. March was set aside for local flying and familiarisation, and the first course began during April. There were six courses altogether, with the last finishing in January 1946.

Instructors and pupils of the first helicopter training course at Andover.
529 Squadron provided the following pupils and Instructors
Back Row from left: F/Lt Houdret (third), F/Lt Turner (sixth), F/Lt Hill (seventh), F/Lt Dennis (eighth)
F/Sgt Wilson (ninth) Instructors front row: F/Lt Harper (first left) F/Lt Bradbury (fourth) F/Lt Ford (fifth)
S/L Basil Arkell is in the centre of the front row (P. Harper Collection)

Sikorsky Hoverfly I KK995 used by 43 OTU at Andover
on display at the RAF Museum at Hendon, London. (DJP)

On the 20th March 1945 three Hoverfly helicopters were delivered to the Royal Aircraft Establishment at Farnborough, Hampshire. They were delivered from Hooton Park, Cheshire with a stop off at Henley. The pilots being S/L Marsh, F/Lt Fry and Lt Hosegood.

Two views of Sikorsky Hoverfly I KK993 'KX-R' of 529 Squadron (Eric Myall Collection)
the lower photograph is probably connected to do with tests for the TRE at Defford.

THE SQUADRON MAKES HISTORY

On April 16th 1945, 529 (Rota) Squadron made history by becoming the first Squadron in the RAF to use helicopters when two Sikorsky R4-B Hoverfly Mk.1's KK993 and KK996, were received from Hooton Park, Cheshire.

The first assignment for one of the helicopters was at Poling, West Sussex on the 27th May for experimental calibration tests of the Chain Home (CH) radar station, with a view of taking over duties from the Avro Rotas.

With the end of the war in Europe the calibration of radar stations became less important and with the departure of the Hoverflys to the AFEE at Beaulieu and TRE at Defford in October 1945, calibrations by 529 Squadron came to an end, the autogiros were gradually disposed of going to 5 Maintenance Unit at RAF Kemble, Gloucestershire from May 1945, several going back into civilian ownership, and the Squadron disbanded during October and November.

Another application involving a 529 Squadron Hoverfly was the testing at Henley of crop-spraying during September 1945 in a joint venture with the Cierva Autogiro Company. The pilots used for these experiments were S/L Marsh and F/Lt Theilmann. The work was then continued at various other sites around Cambridgeshire and Lincolnshire during 1946 and altogether a total of 25 hours of flying were accumulated during the tests.

Sikorsky Hoverfly's used by 529 (Rota) Squadron

KK993   (ex 43-46563)

6th October 1944	Accepted
9th October	Delivered to Floyd Bennett Field, Newark, USA
17th January 1945	Arrived at Martin Hearn Ltd (No. 7 Aircraft Assembly Unit), Hooton Park
13th February	Taken on charge by the RAF
27th February	48 Maintenance Unit, Hawarden for storage
16th April	Collected from Hooton Park
19th April	Transferred to 529 Squadron coded 'KX-R'
27th May	To RNAS Ford for experimental calibration of Poling radar, Sussex
29th September	Displayed at the ATA closing Pageant at White Waltham
30th October	Flown to Defford for use by the Telecommunications Research Establishment
	Loaned to R.A.E. Farnborough from May-June 1946 and again
	from December to January 1947
15th August 1947	damaged at Defford
10th February 1948	Martin Hearn Ltd, Hooton Park, Cheshire for survey
20th April	RNAS Gosport, Hampshire and taken on charge by the Royal Navy
3rd May	705 Squadron, Gosport,
28th September	Struck off charge and used for spares

KK996   (ex 43-46559)

18th October 1944	Accepted
20th October	Delivered to Floyd Bennett Field, Newark, USA
December	Arrived at Martin Hearn Ltd (No. 7 Aircraft Assembly Unit), Hooton Park
13th February 1945	Taken on charge by the RAF
27th February	48 Maintenance Unit, Hawarden for storage
16th April	Collected from Hooton Park, Cheshire
19th April	Transferred to 529 Squadron
2nd May	Demonstrated to C-in-C of Fighter Command
29th October	AFEE, Beaulieu for performance tests arrived here 9th November
circa October 1946	Loaned to British Pictorial Productions, involved in filming ocean liner
	Queen Elizabeth following completion of conversion from a troop carrier
7th March 1947	AFEE, Beaulieu until 23rd March
6th May 1948	Transferred to Royal Navy at Gosport, Hampshire
28th June	Surplus to requirements and struck off charge and used for spares

Hoverfly I KK993 'KX-R' being flown by F/Lt Maurice Houdret
(Peter Durrant)

Airborne Forces Experimental Establishment (AFEE), Beaulieu, Hampshire
Hoverflys were used here for performance tests relating to pilot training, demonstrations and specialised trials which included take-offs and landings, determination of weight and centre of gravity limits, blind flying and performance measurements.

Telecommunications Research Establishment (TRE), Defford, Worcestershire
Hoverflys were used for radio and radar calibration and simulated the flight of a balloon for radio calibration by having a slow rate of climb and downwind draft, and had a large ball hung underneath the helicopter to collect data from the radar response at heights between 400 and 6,000 feet for radar calibrations.

Royal Aircraft Establishment (R.A.E.), Farnborough, Hampshire
KK993 was used here by the Structure and Mechanical Engineering Flight (SME) mainly for stress experiments and pilot training.

Pilots and Ground Crew of 529 (Rota) Squadron

Pilots and Ground Crew with Autogiro DR624

Pilots and Ground Crew, Peter Durrants father who was an Engine Sergeant is standing, hands on hips in white overalls next to 'KX-E,' Autogiro DR622 'KX-X' is visible along with 'KX-O' (Peter Durrant)

Avro Rota I DR624 at Aldenham airfield, Hertfordshire on 6th April 1945
on the left is Air Marshal Sir Roderic Hill the C-in-C of Fighter Command at the time.
The pilot is believed to be F/Lt George Ford (RTR Collection)

Pilots of 529 (Rota) Squadron at Halton circa 1943
Back Row, F/O Jimmy Harper, F/O Norman Hill, F/O ?, F/O John Dennis, F/O Ford,
F/O Jack Gillies, F/O 'Kiwi' Eade
Front Row, F/Lt Walsh, F/Lt Guy Turner, S/L Marsh, F/Lt Maurice Houdret, F/O Dunn (Eng.Off)
(Photo: The Trenchard Museum, RAF Halton)

Squadron Leader Henry Alan Marsh

Alan Marsh was an assistant pilot and later Chief Instructor for Cierva Autogiros and the Cierva School at Hanworth, joining them in April 1932. The School taught many of the pilots who later joined the RAF to fly the Autogiro. Joining the RAF he became the Commander of the Autogiro Radar Calibration Squadron, which was later renumbered 529 (Rota) Squadron where he was the Squadron Leader, (his signature appears on the operations record). He later became Chief Test Pilot on the Cierva W.9 which was tested at Henley. After the war he returned to Cierva where he became the General Manager for the company, he also became the first chairman of the Helicopter Association of Great Britain. He returned to test flying and during the testing of the Cierva Air Horse on the 13th June 1950 was killed when it crashed at Eastleigh, near Southampton.

John Norman Dennis

In 1938 he joined the RAFVR and Served with No 3 and No 139 Squadrons. In 1942 joined the Autogyro (Flight) at Halton. On the 23rd December 1943 he crashed taking off from Kenley in Hornet Moth W9387 with F/O Smith as passenger although both escaped unhurt the aircraft was badly damaged. From the 27th March 1944 he was attached to 528 Squadron at Filton near Bristol for Flying Duties. He was then at 60 Group from the 9th to the 11th of April 1944 before returning to 528 Squadron on the 21st, before moving again to 527 for 28 days on the 11th August, he then moved to 529 Squadron. He went to 43 OTU for a Helicopter Conversion Course and then joined the RAE. On the 19th August 1948 when flying Hoverfly I KL109 whilst photographing a Halifax container drop, he experienced a major problem with a blade and crashed at Buckland near Brize Norton without serious injury. In 1949 he was appointed as rotating wing test pilot to the Fairey Aviation Co's Rotorcraft Division.

Philip P. Godfrey

Posted to 529 Squadron on 2nd February 1944 for Flying Duties from 286 Squadron at Weston Zoyland, Somerset where he had been flying Boulton-Paul Defiants.

James (Jimmy) Edgar Harper (AFC)

May 1935 – August 1935, Uxbridge
August 1935 –September 1938, Kenley
September 1938 – February 1939, 17 Squadron, Kenley
February 1939 – July 1939, 17 Squadron, North Weald
July 1939 – October 1939, 22 EFTS, Cambridge flying Tiger Moths (Initially as a Corporal)
October 1939 – April 1940, 14 FTS, Kinloss flying the North American Harvard
April 1940 – August 1940, Odiham, Autogyro Training Flight
August 1940 - December 1940, Duxford, No 76 (S) Wing
December 1940 – March 1941, Filton, No 76 (S) Wing
April 1941, Duxford, C.30 refresher, Autogyro Section, No 74 Wing
March 1942, Halton, 1448 Flight.
June 1943 Halton, 529 Squadron (Flew many duals with new pilots.)
25th February 1946 Posted to AFEE Beaulieu, "B" Flight
10th July 1946 Experienced tail rotor failure in Hoverfly I KK974 when flying from Beaulieu at night although he escaped unhurt
Flight of 9th October 1947 says "Flying a Sikorski S.51 owned by Pest Control"

Norman Hill

Was a pre-war Chief Technical Officer at British Electric Traction Co. and had considerable autogiro experience. After the war he became the manager of Tecalemit Ltd aircraft division.

Maurice S. P. Houdret

He was the Secretary of Redhill Flying Club, Surrey pre-war and Bought a C.30 which was impressed into RAF service. When the Police interest in aviation began, he became an unpaid Sergeant in the Reigate Special Constabulary. It is Possible he returned to Redhill after the war.

John Graham Theilmann

Flew Spitfires with 41 Squadron at Catterick around 1940. Post war from 1947 he was senior pilot of BEA Experimental Helicopter Unit under W/Cdr Reggie Brie. The Unit moved from Yeovil to Westwood, Peterborough in May 1948.

Guy Cecil Turner

Pre-war was a "stockjobber" (a person dealing in stocks) and learned to fly a Cierva C.30 at Hanworth.

The following are listed in the operations record for the Squadron
rank and name plus identity number and the types of aircraft they flew are listed where known.

Flight Sergeant G. C. Banks - *Hornet Moth*

Warrant Officer R. Davidson - *Rota, Hornet Moth, Oxford*

Flight Lieutenant John Norman Dennis (134496) - *Rota, Hornet Moth*

Flying Lieutenant Edward Eason - *Rota*

Flight Lieutenant George A.'Henry' Ford (51164) - *Rota*

Flight Lieutenant L. E. 'Jack' Gillies (149365) - *Oxford, Rota, Hornet Moth, Hoverfly*

Flight Lieutenant Philip P. Godfrey (88393) - *Hornet Moth, Oxford*

Flight Lieutenant Norman Hill - *Hornet Moth, Rota, Oxford, Hoverfly*

Flight Lieutenant Maurice S. P. Houdret (89052) - *Oxford, Rota, Hoverfly*

Squadron Leader H. A. Marsh (70446) - *Oxford, Hoverfly*

Flight Lieutenant J. K. Newman (49873) - *Oxford*

Flight Lieutenant A. E. Polden (116131) - *Oxford*

Flying Officer R. G. Read (149516) - *Rota, Hornet Moth, Oxford*

Flight Lieutenant O. Roberts (186708) - *Rota, Hoverfly, Oxford*

Flying Officer Peter D. Smith - *Rota*

Squadron Leader John Graham Theilmann (37701) - *Oxford, Rota, Hornet Moth, Hoverfly*

Flight Lieutenant Guy Cecil Turner (83211) - *Oxford, Rota*

Flying Officer Wilson - *Hornet Moth, Oxford*

Flight Lieutenant Young - *Oxford*

The following are also listed as pilots with the Squadron, or trained as instructors with 43 OTU
Flight Lieutenant R. Bradbury, Flight Lieutenant Eade, Flight Lieutenant James 'Jimmy' E. Harper,
Flight Lieutenant R. J. Miller, Flight Sergeant W. D. Milne, Flying Officer Denys Michael White,
Flight Lieutenant Wilkinson, S/L Keith Jefferson Henderson

Pilots and Ground Crew at Halton circa 1943 (photo via: Francis Hanford)

One member of the ground crew posted to 529 Squadron at Henley was Brian Hughes, he arrived in
Henley at the railway station, then took a taxi to the airfield, he was amongst the first of the small advance
party. Here he found a row of empty huts, he got in contact with RAF Shinfield Park, Reading for food
rations and also transport, then settled the party for the arrival of S/L Marsh.

The Following is taken from (AIR 27/2000) from The National Archives, Kew
This is from the operations record book of 529 Squadron and covers the period when the squadron was based at Henley-on-Thames

OPERATIONS RECORD BOOK

R.A.F. Form 540

see instructions for use of this form in K.R and A.C.I.
para 2349 and War Manual Pt. II., chapter XX, and
notes in R.A.F. Pocket Book.

of (Unit or Formation) No 529 (Rota) Squadron

Summary of Events

Orders from HQ 60 Group to be at "Readiness" for move in six hours as from noon tomorrow. No information as to where to go.
12th August 1944 Conference at Group at 09.00 to discuss move. Various places suggested but definite instructions awaited.

15th August Halton
10.00 hours
Conference at RAF Henley between HQ 60 Group, Flying Training Command, HQ 50 Group, Messrs Phillips & Powis Ltd (Woodley) No.529 Squadron. re move of Squadron, details refers Squadron moving as from 16/8/44. Move will be completed by 19/8/44.
F/Lt Hill attached from HQ 60 Group to assist in taking over Henley and organising the move etc.

16th August Halton
08.00 hours
Advance party of one officer (F/Lt Houdret) and 27 NCO's and airmen left Halton for Henley.
14.00 hours
Eight Hornet Moths, Ten C30 Rotas and one Tiger Moth flown to Henley.
One Oxford and one Hornet Moth left at Halton and three C30 Rotas and one Hornet Moth on detachments
Total of twenty five aircraft in all.
G/Capt Cardale SOA 60 Group visited Halton re move
14.30 hours
F/Lt Hill in Hornet Moth W5777 to Valley for the T.R.E experimental work in conjunction with Rota BV999.

18th August Halton
13.00 hours
Main party of airmen and stores left Halton for Henley. Pilots flown over and only three officers left at Halton, C.O., Adjutant and Engineering Officer.
Oxford aircraft flown over to Henley
17.00 hours
F/O Eason Avro Rota K4233 to Henley from Christchurch having completed azimuth calibration of Southbourne, 78 Wing

19th August Halton
13.00 hours
Rear party left Halton for Henley. All buildings at Halton handed over C.O., Adjutant and Engineering Officer left for Henley and remaining aircraft and Hornet Moth flown over.
15.45 hours Henley
Move completed and signal sent to HQ 60 Group.

<u>SECRET</u>

1st September
Aircraft strength as at 1/9 is 25 (13 C30 Rota, 1 Tiger Moth, 1 Oxford, 10 Hornet Moths)

4th September
G/Capt Cardale 60 Group visited Station late pm

5th September p.m.
F/Lt Godfrey ceased attachment to T.R.E. for interview with AOC

6th September p.m.
F/Lt Harper, F/O's Dennis, Ford and Eade attached to No 5 pre F.I.S, (Theale)
for instructors course w/e 6/9

7th September a.m.
Rota K4239 ferried from Hanworth ex loan to M.A.P.

8th September a.m.
F/O Read Rota HM580 to Exeter for azimuth calibration of Branscombe, (78 Wing)

9th September a.m.
Photographic work carried out for War Office Film Unit

12th September p.m.
AOC's Oxford T1210 collected from Station Flight at Halton to be based at Henley

19th September a.m.
AOC's Oxford T1210 S/L Marsh and S/L Theilmann to Wing to pick up AOC for France.
arrived B17 (Carpiquet) at 13.00 hrs

20th September (B17) p.m.
Left B17, for Brussels arriving 15.30 hours

21st September Brussels a.m.
Left Brussels for B17 arriving 13.00 hours
Left B17 for Wing arriving 17.40 hours aircraft then returned to base (Henley)

23rd September a.m.
S/L Henderson posted to the Squadron supernumerary pending disposal
(ex 528 Squadron)

30th September p.m.
F/Lt Godfrey Hornet Moth WS830 to Hawkinge for azimuth calibration of Rye,
75 Wing
S/L Marsh and F/Lt Houdret Oxford T1210 to Brussels collect Group Captain Phillips
O/C 72 Wing

Total flying hours for the month: 142 hours 25 minutes

O.C. No. 529 (ROTA) SQUADRON
R. A. F.

Azimuth - Arc of sky from zenith to horizon

1st October p.m.
S/L Marsh and F/Lt Houdret Oxford T1210 returned from Brussels and Chievre with Group Captain Phillips

2nd October a.m.
F/O Read Rota HM580 from Exeter having completed Branscombe 78 Wing
Rota K4239 ferried to Contractors for major overhaul
Rota BV999 ferried to base from Valley having completed work with T.R.E.
F/O Newman promoted to F/Lt w/e 31/5

5th October p.m.
Further photographic work carried out for War Office job, work completed

7th October a.m. & p.m.
S/L Theilmann and F/O Gillies to Wing en route Chievre with 60 Group Officers pax Oxford T1210
F/O P. D. Smith re posted to the Squadron from 527 Squadron

11th October a.m. & p.m.
F/Lt Houdret Rota AP506 to Horsham St.Faith for work with 5th AA Group
S/L Theilmann and F/O Gillies returned from Brussels via Wing Oxford T1210

12th October a.m.
S/L Marsh and F/Lt Newman left for Wing to convey AOC to Brussels in Oxford T1210

14th October a.m. & p.m.
F/O Gillies Rota V1187 left for Christchurch for azimuth calibration of Southbourne, 78 Wing
S/L Marsh and F/Lt Newman returned from Brussels with AOC

18th October p.m.
F/Lt Bradbury posted supernumerary ex Helicopter Course in USA

24th October
14.00 Hours
F/O Eason Rota K4233 left for Charterhall for azimuth calibration of Drone Hill, 70 Wing
F/O Read Rota HM580 left for Brough for calibration of AA sector 5th AA Brigade

27th October
12.30 hours
S/L Theilmann Rota AP510 to Ouston for calibration of AA sector in Newcastle area 5th AA
14.00 hours
F/Lt Houdret Rota AP506 to base from Horsham St.Faith having temporarily completed AA calibration in Norfolk area 5th AA Brigade
14.30 hours
Air Com. Hewat (P.M.O. of F.T.C.) carried out an inspection of the station

28th October
15.00 hours
F/O Smith Rota K4232 to Ipswich for calibration of AA site

Total flying hours for the month: 152 hours 05 minutes

O.C. No. 529 (ROTA) SQUADRON
R. A. F.   1/11/1944

105

1st November
Aircraft and pilots detached
F/O Eason Rota K4233 Charterhall for calibration of Drone Hill, 70 Wing
F/O Gillies Rota V1187 Christchurch for calibration of Southbourne, 78 Wing
S/L Theilmann Rota AP510 Ouston for calibration of AA sites, 5th AA
F/O Read Rota HM580 Brough for calibration of AA sites, 5th AA
F/O Smith Rota K4232 Ipswich for calibration of AA sites, 1st AA

4th November a.m.
F/O J. N. Dennis promoted to F/Lt w/e 2/11
F/O Houdret Rota AP506 to Ipswich for calibration of AA sites, 1st AA

6th November
17.00 hours
F/O Eason Rota K4233 to base from Charterhall having completed azimuth calibration
of Drone Hill, 70 Wing

7th November
09.00 hours
F/Lts Newman and Turner to Wing and Chievre on communications work for
HQ 60 Group, Oxford T1210

9th November
11.00 hours
F/Lt Newman and Turner to base from Chievre, Oxford T1210

10th November
S/L Theilmann Rota AP510 moved from Ouston to Thornaby to continue with
AA Calibration

15th November
S/L Henderson posted to No.7 (FIS) Upavon for Instructors Course
F/O Gillies Rota V1187 moved from Christchurch to Roborough for azimuth calibration
of Downderry, 78 Wing
F/Lt Houdret Rota AP506 moved from Ipswich to Detling to continue calibration
of AA sites, 1st AA Group

16th November
F/O Read Rota HM580 moving from Brough to Horsham St.Faith for work with
AA 5th Group

17th November a.m.
F/Lt Hill proceeded to Ipswich to take over from F/O Smith, latter due for
repatriation to Canada
cancel entry re F/Lt Houdret 15/11
F/Lt Hill will proceed from Ipswich to Detling with Rota K4232
F/Lt Houdret remains at Ipswich

20th November
F/O Smith posted to R.C.A.F.' R' Depot Warrington for repatriation to Canada

21st November
F/Lt Hill Rota K4232 arrived at Detling from Ipswich
F/O Read Rota HM580 arrived at Horsham St.Faith from Brough Both pilots have been
delayed by weather

23rd November
S/L Theilmann Rota APsio returned to Ouston from Thornaby to continue AA calibration 5th Group

27th November p.m.
Rota K4235 ferried from contractor after overhaul

29th November p.m.
F/O Gillies Rota V1187 to base from Roborough for aircraft change and special gear adjustments

30th November p.m.
F/O Eason Rota K4233 to Hawkinge for Azimuth calibration of Rye, 75 Wing

31st November p.m.
S/L Theilmann Rota APsio returned to base from Ouston having completed AA calibration for 5th AA Group

Total flying time for the month: 183 hours 5 minutes

O.C. No. 529 (ROTA) SQUADRON
R. A. F.   1/12/1944

2nd December a.m.
F/O Gillies Rota DR622 to Roborough to complete azimuth calibration of Downderry
F/Lt Godfrey Hornet Moth W5749 to Ipswich for work with 9th AA Group

4th December p.m.
F/O D M White posted for flying duties ex Middle East along with W/O R Davidson,
F/Sgt G G Banks and F/Sgt W D Milne

5th December p.m.
Station visited by G/Capt Appleyard. Chaplain other denominations

6th December a.m.
F/Sgts Banks and Milne attached to No.526 Squadron Inverness for flying duties
Instructions HQ 60 Group

7th December p.m.
F/O's Ford and Eason promoted to F/Lts w/e 14/11
F/Lt Houdret Rota AP506 to base from Ipswich – AA Calibrations
F/Lt Eason Rota K4233 to base from Hawkinge having completed azimuth calibration
of Rye, 75 Wing

9th December p.m.
G/Capt Weston G.T.O. Fighter Command visited the Station p.m.

11th December a.m.
F/Lt Dennis to Horsham St.Faith to release F/O Read, latter returning to unit

12th December p.m.
F/Lt Eason Rota AP510 to Hawkinge for azimuth calibration of Swingate,
75 Wing

18th December p.m.
F/O Read Rota BV999 to Manby for azimuth hits with Stenigot, 75 Wing

21st December p.m.
F/O Gillies Rota DR622 to base from Roborough having completed azimuth calibration of
Downderry, 78 Wing

22nd December p.m.
F/O Read Rota BV999 to base from Manby, work at Stenigot postponed

23rd December p.m.
F/Lt Godfrey Hornet Moth W5749 to base from Ipswich, work with 9th AA Group
postponed for a time

27th December p.m.
S/L Theilmann to Hawkinge to relieve F/Lt Eason. latter returning to base

31st December p.m.
F/Lt Godfrey Hornet Moth W5749 to Ipswich for work with 9th AA Group

F/Lt Dennis removed from FIS Woodley returned to Squadron w/e 6/12/44

Flying times for the month: 124 hours 15 minutes

O.C. No. 529 (ROTA) SQUADRON
R. A. F.   1/1/1945

1st January 1945
Aircraft and pilots on detachment
F/Lt Dennis Rota HM580 Horsham St.Faith 5th AA Group
F/Lt Godfrey Hornet Moth W5749 Ipswich 9th AA Group
F/Lt Hill Rota K4232 Detling 9th AA Group
F/Lt Houdret Rota BV999 Manby for Stenigot, 75 Wing
S/L Theilmann Rota AP510 Hawkinge for Swingate, 75 Wing

1st January
S/L H A Marsh awarded Air Force Cross in New Year Honours List

3rd January
F/O D M White awarded the Distinguished Flying Cross for operations in the Middle East
F/Lt Dennis Rota HM580 from Horsham St.Faith for aircraft exchange p.m.

5th January p.m.
F/O Gillies Rota AP506 to Brough for work with 5th AA Group

11th January
F/Lt R J Miller posted supernumerary from 527 Squadron

15th January p.m.
F/Lt Dennis Rota DR623 to Horsham St.Faith for work with 5th AA
F/Lt J. Harper " Mentioned in Despatches" in New Years Honours List

17th January a.m.
Rota HM581 flown out to contractor for major overhaul
F/Lt Hill Rota K4232 to base from Detling having completed work for 9th AA

22nd January
F/Lt Bradbury posted to 43 OTU Andover to open Helicopter Training Flight

23rd January
F/O White DFC posted to No 17 OTU Silverstone for operational training

24th January
F/Lt Miller posted to No 15 AFU Babdown Farm for conversion training
P/O O Roberts posted for flying duties ex tour of operations with No 69 Squadron

27th January p.m.
F/Lt Godfrey Hornet Moth W5749 to base having completed AA work at Ipswich

Rota K4233 to Hawkinge as relief aircraft for Rota AP510 latter to base
F/Lts Harper, Ford and Eade completed Elementary Instructors Course at No 10 FIS
on 12/1/45 and returned to Unit pending disposal

Flying time for month: 114 hours 15 minutes

O.C. No. 529 (ROTA) SQUADRON
R. A. F.   1/2/1945

1st February a.m.
Station visited by G/Capt Jarvis CDO 60 Group re Defence matters

2nd February
F/Lts Harper, Ford and Eade posted to No 43 OTU for conversion as Helicopter
instructors w/e 2/2

3rd February a.m.
F/Lt Eades posting to 43 OTU cancelled. Posted to 12 RNZAF (PDRC) for repatriation
to New Zealand w/e 5/2
F/O Read Rota HM580 to Friston for azimuth calibration of Pevensey, 75 Wing
AVM Edmonds AOC F.T.C. visited Station on taking up appointment p.m.

5th February
F/Lt Eason posted to 12 RNZAF (PDRC) for repatriation to New Zealand w/e 7/5

8th February a.m.
F/Lt Dennis Rota DR623 to base from Horsham St.Faith.
Returning to Horsham with Hornet Moth to continue work for AA

9th February a.m.
F/Lt Dennis Hornet Moth WS830 to Horsham St.Faith to continue work with 5th AA

10th February p.m.
S/L Theilmann Rota K4233 to base from Hawkinge work at Swingate suspended

20th February p.m.
F/O Gillies Rota APS06 to base from Brough to exchange Rota a/c for Hornet Moth
F/Lt Dennis Hornet Moth WS830 returned from Horsham St.Faith, AA calibration
temporarily suspended

21st February a.m.
F/O Gillies Hornet Moth W9389 to Brough for work with 5th AA

23rd February p.m.
F/O Wilson posted to this unit from No 526 Squadron for flying duties

24th February p.m.
F/O Valentine posted from 73 Wing for Adjutant's duties

25th February p.m.
F/Sgt Banks (Pilot) returned from attachment at No 526 Squadron
Oxford T1210 to Wing for AOC's trip to Chievre, cancelled due to weather outlook for
tomorrow

27th February a.m. & p.m.
S/L Theilmann Hornet Moth WS777 to Brough for work with 5th AA Group
F/Lt Houdret Rota BV999 to base from Manby work with 5th AA Group completed
W/O Davidson Rota APS07 crashed on landing at Henley on a training flight.
Aircraft repaired at unit. Pilot unhurt

Flying time for the month: 151 hours 25 minutes

O.C. No. 529 (ROTA) SQUADRON
R. A. F.   1/3/1945

4th March a.m.
S/L Marsh and F/Lt Hill Oxford T1210 to Chievre to bring back AVM Theak
Hornet Moth W9383 ferried to Friston for F/O Read to carry out azimuth calibration
"checks" on Pevensey

6th March p.m.
S/L Marsh and F/Lt Hill Oxford T1210 to base having returned from Chievre to Wing
with AVM Theak
F/Lt Godfrey Hornet Moth W5749 to Brough to release S/L Theilmann,
5th AA Calibration work
F/O Fulton posted to HQ Transport Command w/e 6/3

8th March p.m.
S/L Theilmann Hornet Moth W5777 to base from Brough
C.O. to conference at Air Ministry re allocation of helicopters to 60 Group
and training of personnel etc.

15th March
S/L Marsh and F/Lt Hill to Ghent (B61) and return with Radar Equipment for
HQ 85 Group

18th March
S/L Theilmann to Brough to release F/O Gillies for AA calibration

19th March
10.08 hours
An incident occurred at 1000 hrs – presumably a V2 – which fell and exploded in a field
approx 50-60 yards from the Technical Site (South) gate of the aerodrome, certain
damage sustained to two hangars and Officers Mess and slight damage to four aircraft
these are repairable on site within 24 hours. But F/Sgt sustained lacerated arm & hand
injuries due to flying glass.
Report rendered HQFTC and HQ 60 Group.

22nd March
15.00 hours
Air Marshal Sir P. Babington AOC in C Flying Training Command visited the Station in
company with AVM Edmonds AOA F.T.C.

26th March p.m.
S/L Theilmann recalled from Brough to take Court of inquiry at 527 Squadron
F/O Wilson proceeding to Brough 27/3 to continue AA work

27th March a.m.
S/L Theilmann W5754, F/O Wilson W5779 proceeded as above
F/O Wilson in Hornet Moth W5779 to Brough to continue AA work

30th March a.m.
F/O Read Rota HM580 and Hornet Moth W5749 returned from Friston having completed
azimuth calibration of Pevensey

Flying time for the month: 227 hours 5 minutes

O.C. No. 529 (ROTA) SQUADRON
R. A. F.   4/4/1945

3rd April
F/Lts Turner, Houdret, Hill and Dennis to 43 OTU Andover for Helicopter Conversion
Course- Six weeks duration

6th April
C-in-C Fighter Command flown from Aldenham to Lacey Green (B.C. Landing Strip)
and returned to Aldenham

8th April
F/O Gillies to Brough to relieve F/Lt Godfrey, latter to base

9th April p.m.
Hornet Moth WS830 to De Havillands, Witney for major overhaul

13th April
New aircraft establishment approved reducing to:
7 Rotas, 5 Hornet Moths, 1 Tiger Moth, 2 Oxfords and 2 Sikorksi R4Bs
Remaining Rotas to be replaced by Sikorskis in due course
8 Rotas, 4 Hornet Moths put up to 43 Group for disposal

14th April a.m.
Rota HM581 collected from contractors after overhaul

16th April p.m.
Sikorski R-4B's KK996 and KK993 collected from Hooton Park

17th April a.m.
S/L Theilmann Rota K4239 to Peterhead for azimuth calibration of Schoolhill, 70 Wing

18th April
10.30 hours
Court Martial held at this station (W/C Taylor, President) on AC1 Connelly of 529 Squadron

19th April
F/Lt Godfrey to Brough to replace F/O Gillies - latter to base

20th April
New establishment of personnel to conform with reduction of aircraft received
Some slight reduction in technical ranks.

23rd April
Oxford T1210 to A84 to collect A/Com Phillips for Hendon

25th April
Oxford X7238 to A84 to take A/Com Phillips to 72 Wing

26th April
Hornet Moths WS777, WS750 and AV952 allotted to 5 MU and flown away

28th April p.m.

Hornet Moth X9310 allotted to De Havillands for overhaul, all surplus Hornet Moths now disposed of

S/L Theilmann Rota K4239 to base from Peterhead having completed azimuth calibration of Schoolhill

F/O Gillies to Brough to replace F/Lt Godfrey on AA calibration. F/Lt Godfrey to base

29th April

Test work carried out with Naval Compass Establishment at Slough

Oxford X7238 fitted with 3106 and UHF for this purpose Series of tests were due to commence in a few days

Flying hours for the month: 198 hours 45 minutes

O.C. No. 529 (ROTA) SQUADRON
R. A. F.   1/5/1945

*The Naval Compass Establishment or the Admiralty Compass Observatory (to give it's proper name) and Radio Research Station was based at Ditton Park near Slough, Berkshire

1st May
Pilots and Aircraft on detachment
F/O Wilson Hornet Moth W5779 Brough, AA Calibration 5th AA Group
F/O Gillies Hornet Moth W9383 Brough, AA Calibration 5th AA Group
W/O Davidson Hornet Moth W9389 Wick for azimuth calibration of Tannach 70 Wing
F/Lt Turner, Houdret, Hill and Dennis detached to Helicopter Training Flight Andover for
Conversion Course

2nd May a.m.
S/L Marsh Helicopter KK996 to Fighter Command for demonstration to C-in-C
Tests with Naval Compass Base, Slough commenced with Oxford a/c.
These tests will continue, weather permitting, for some days until completed.

8th May
VE Day, Station closed for the day except for essential services

10th May
Oxford T1210 to Chievre (A84) to collect Air/Com Phillips

11th May p.m.
P/O Roberts Rota K4235 to Ford for azimuth calibration of Poling, 75 Wing

12th May p.m.
Oxford T1210 to Hendon and Chievre (A84) to take Air/Com Phillips
F/O Gillies and F/O Wilson Hornet Moth W5779 to base from Brough
F/Sgt Banks to Brough to continue AA calibration with Hornet Moth

13th May a.m.
F/Lts Turner, Houdret, Hill and Dennis to unit having completed
Helicopter Conversion Course

15th May a.m.
Seven Rota aircraft flown to 5 MU Kemble for storage

16th May a.m.
F/Lt J. N. Dennis posted to AFEE Beaulieu
F/Lt Godfrey, F/O Read and F/O Gillies attached to Helicopter Training Flight
Andover for Conversion Course

17th May
S/L Theilmann took over command vice S/L Marsh on leave until 22/5

18th May Mons/Belgium a.m. & p.m.
G/Capt Wilson and F/Lt Mansell (HQ 60 Gp) conveyed to Mons (72 Wing) in Oxford T1210
by S/L Theilmann. S/L Theilmann and F/Lt Mansell proceeded by air to Brussels (Evere)
for the night

19th May a.m. Belgium/Holland
F/O Read proceeded to Helicopter Training Flight at Andover
S/L Theilmann and F/Lt Mansell proceeded from Evere to B.106 (Henglo) via B.91 (Nijmegen)
in Oxford T1210. F/Lt Mansell dropped at B.106, S/L Theilmann returned to base via Evere
(B.56) and Chievre (A.84) picking up F/Lt Jones at Chievre for return to UK from 72 Wing
Mons.

Summary of Events

20th May
All AA calibration cooperation terminated. F/Sgt Banks and crew recalled from Brough.

21st May
Azimuth calibration of Poling by P/O Roberts completed. P/O Roberts returned to base in autogiro K4235 P.M.

23rd May
S/L Marsh assumed command of 529 Squadron vice S/L Theilmann

27th May a.m. & p.m.
S/L Theilmann Oxford T1210 to A84 (Chievre) and return to collect G/Capt Wilson
F/Lt Houdret Sikorski R4B KK993 to Ford for experimental calibration of Poling

28th May
P/O Roberts promoted " Flying Officer" w/e 5/4 auth London Gazette 11/5
S/L Henderson DFC reported on posting supernumerary ex 526 Squadron. w/e 25/5

29th May a.m.
Rota AP506 allotted and flown in to s MU Kemble

Flying time for the month: 166 hours 40 minutes

O.C. No. 529 (ROTA) SQUADRON
R. A. F.   1/ 6/ 1945

1. Location: 529 (R) Sqdn. R.A.F. Station, Upper Culham Farm, Wargrave, Nr. Reading.
2. Type: Half Nissen Hut for M.I. & Crash Room.
3. ESTABLISHMENT: One N.C.O. (Cpl). 4 N/Orderlies.
4. Actual Staff: 1238856 Cpl. Skinner. E.M. (Attached)
                  1095955 LAC. Thomas. A.
                  1239843 LAC. Pickup. R.S. (Attached)

Periodic Sanitary Inspection carried out by,
F/Lt C. M. Carr. (F.T.C.) Woodley

Cm Carr F/Lt.
Officer in Medical Charge. -5 JUN 1945

529 (R) Sqdn, R.A.F. Station
Henley, Berks

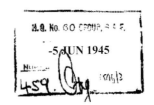

1st June
Pilots and Aircraft on detachment
F/Lt Houdret Sikorski Helicopter KK993 at Ford for Poling 75 Wing
W/O Davidson in Hornet Moth W9389 at Wick for Tannach 75 Wing
F/Lt Godfrey, F/O's Read and Gillies at Andover for Helicopter Conversion Course

14th June a.m.
F/Lt Houdret Sikorski Helicopter KK993 to base having completed first phase
of experiments at Poling
F/Lt Turner in Rota AP509 to Ford for azimuth check runs at Poling

15th June
F/Lt Turner Rota AP509 to Ford on the 15/6 and return to base on 22/6 to check
results on Poling obtained by Helicopter

22nd June a.m. & p.m.
F/O Wilson Oxford X7238 to Wing to convey W/Cdr Jennings to Schleswig
on attachment
F/Lt Houdret Helicopter KK993 to Ford to continue work with Poling
W/O Davidson Hornet Moth W9389 to base from Wick having completed work with
Tannach

27th June p.m.
F/Lt Godfrey and F/O Read and Gillies to unit after Helicopter Conversion Course at
Andover
S/L Theilmann, F/Lt Newman and F/O Roberts to Helicopter Training Flight, Andover
for Conversion Course. w/e 9/5
F/O Read promoted to the rank of F/Lt and awarded the "Air Efficiency Award"
F/Lt Houdret awarded "Mentioned in Despatches" London Gazette 14/6/45

Flying time for the month: 138 hours 15 Minutes

O.C. No. 529 (ROTA) SQUADRON
R. A. F.   1/7/1945

H.Q. No. 60 GROUP. R.A.F.

4 JUL 1945

459.

1st July
Pilots and aircraft on detachment
F/Lt Houdret Helicopter KK993 at Ford for Poling 75 Wing
S/L Theilmann, F/Lt Newman and F/O Roberts at Andover for Helicopter Conversion Course
F/O Wilson Oxford X7238 at Schleswig for HQ 60 Group

3rd July a.m.
F/Lts Godfrey and Read Oxford T1210 to Le Bourget for HQ 60 Group
F/Lt Houdret Helicopter KK993 to base from Ford. Poling closing down for two weeks

5th July a.m.
F/Lts Godfrey and Read Oxford T1210 to base from Le Bourget

7th July p.m.
F/O Wilson Oxford X7238 from Schleswig with W/C Jennings 60 Group

19th July p.m.
F/Lt Hill Helicopter KK993 to Tangmere to continue work with Poling, 75 Wing

21st July p.m.
Hornet Moth W5749 flown to Inverness 70 Wing aircraft on loan to detached flight 527 Squadron

31st July p.m.
F/Lt Hill Helicopter KK993 to base from Tangmere for 60 hour aircraft inspection

Flying time for the month: 110 hours 35 minutes

O.C. No. 529 (ROTA) SQUADRON
R. A. F.

1st August
Aircraft and pilots on detachments
Hornet Moth WS749 on loan to 527 Squadron Inverness
S/L Theilmann, F/Lt Newman and F/O Roberts at Andover for Helicopter Conversion Course

3rd August p.m.
Oxford X7238 F/O Gillies and F/Lt Godfrey to Le Bourget for HQ 60 Group

4th August a.m.
Oxford X7238 F/O Gillies and F/Lt Godfrey from Le Bourget

7th August p.m.
S/L Theilmann, F/Lt Newman and F/O Roberts returned to unit on completion of Helicopter Conversion Course, Andover

8th August a.m.
F/O Gillies Helicopter KK993 to Tangmere for work with Poling
F/Lts Turner, Houdret and Godfrey and F/O Wilson posted to 100 PDC for release

18th August
F/O Gillies promoted to F/Lt w/e 4/6

20th August a.m.
F/Lt Polden posted for flying duties from ACAC

21st August p.m.
F/Lt Young posted for flying duties from ACAC

23rd August a.m. & p.m.
S/L Theilmann to Tangmere to relieve F/Lt Gillies
F/Lt Wilkinson posted for flying duties from ACAC Catterick

30th August p.m.
S/L Theilmann Helicopter KK993 to base from Tangmere

31st August p.m.
W/O Davidson Rota K4235 to Ipswich for special Calibration work for HQ 60 Group

Total flying time for the month: 107 hours 20 minutes

O.C. No. 529 (ROTA) SQUADRON
R. A. F.

529 (Rota) Squadron

1st September
W/O Davidson Rota K4235 at Woodbridge for special Calibration work
F/Lts Hill, Newman and Read to 100 PDC Uxbridge for demobilisation
S/L Theilmann and F/Lt Polden Oxford T1210 to Wing and Brussels
with AOC and P.a. on 1/9 and return to base on 2/9

3rd September a.m.
W/O Davidson Rota K4235 to base from Woodbridge

6th September a.m.
F/O Roberts Helicopter KK993 to Tangmere to continue work with Poling
S/L Theilmann and F/Lt Polden Oxford T1210 to Brussels for AOC

7th September p.m.
S/L Theilmann and F/Lt Polden Oxford T1210 to base from Brussels with AOC and P.a.
F/Lt G. C. Turner (since released) awarded Air Force Cross

10th September
Tests carried out live for N.P.L. in connection with D.F. using Sikorski fitted
with transmitter

12th September a.m.
F/Lt Wilkinson attached to HQ 60 Group for Victory Parade

14th September a.m.
F/O Roberts Helicopter KK993 from Tangmere to base having completed azimuth
calibration of Poling, 75 Wing

15th September a.m.
F/Lt Polden and F/Lt Young Oxford T1210 to Bad Eilsen for HQ 60 Group

16th September a.m.
F/Lt Polden and F/Lt Young Oxford T1210 returned to base from Bad Eilsen

19th September p.m.
Tiger Moth T6864 ferried to Digby on loan to 527 Squadron
S/L Henderson, F/Lt Polden and W/O Banks attached to Helicopter Training Flight
at Andover for conversion course

21st September a.m.
F/Lt Gillies Helicopter KK993 to Defford for TRE

23rd September a.m.
F/O Roberts and W/O Davidson to Wing, Brussels and return to base for HQ 60 Group

26th September a.m.
F/Lt Gillies Helicopter KK993 to base from Defford

27th September
Tests continued and completed for N.P.L. re D.F. work

Total flying time for the month: 101 hours 30 minutes

O.C. No. 529 (ROTA) SQUADRON
R. A. F.

1st October
Pilots on attachment
S/L Henderson, F/Lt Polden and W/O Banks, Andover

2nd October a.m.
S/L Theilmann and F/Lt Gillies Oxford T1210 to Brussels and return for HQ 60 Group

5th October
F/Lt Gillies posted to AFEE Beaulieu for flying duties

19th October
Tiger Moth T6864 returned from loan to 527 Squadron

22nd October
Hornet Moth W5749 returned from loan to Inverness

29th October p.m.
Sikorski Helicopters KK993 and KK996 allotted to TRU, Defford and
AFEE, Beaulieu respectively and collected by pilots from AFEE.

Unofficial news received during month of disbandment of Squadron
Official notification awaited from Group.

Flying time for the month: 56 hours 45 minutes

O.C. No. 529 (ROTA) SQUADRON
R. A. F.

H.Q. No. 60 GROUP, R A F.

2 NOV 1945

1st November
Aircraft on strength
5 Hornet Moths, 1 Tiger Moth, 2 Oxfords and 7 Rotas
Pilots on strength
3 S/Ls, 7 F/Lts, 1 F/O and 2 W/Os
(1 S/L, 1 F/Lt and 1 W/O attached to Andover for Helicopter course

9th November
F/Lt Wilkinson and F/O Roberts posted to 100 PDC for release

10th November
Tiger Moth T6864 allotted to 9 MU at Cosford and delivered by air

12th November
Autogiros AP509, K4239 and DR623 allotted to 5 MU Kemble and delivered by air

13th November
Autogiros DR624, K4235 and HM581 allotted to 5 MU Kemble and delivered by air

16th November
Hornet Moths W9383 and W9389 allotted and flown to 5 MU Kemble

26th November
Hornet Moths W5749, W5779 and W5754 and Autogiro HM580 allotted and flown into 5 MU Kemble

27th November
Oxford X7238 allotted and flown into 12 MU Kirkbride

Note: All aircraft now disposed of.
Instruction still awaited for disposal of technical stores and equipment together with barrack equipment etc.

No further entries

O.C. No. 529 (ROTA) SQUADRON
R. A. F.

RADAR SITES MAP

Locations of RAF Chain Home (CH) radar stations and airfield bases used for calibrations
by 529 (Rota) Squadron from August 1944.

CHAIN HOME RADAR

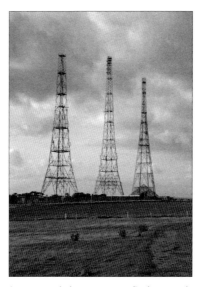

Chain Home radar transmitting masts at Swingate situated above the
cliffs at Dover on the English south coast. (Bob Cromwell)

A minor experiment in a field at Daventry in February 1935 demonstrated that aircraft could be detected by radio waves. The experiment grew directly from the need to prove, that if an aircraft was 'picked-up' by radio waves, then it could be reflected to permit detection on the ground. Tests were then carried out at Orford Ness in Suffolk between 1935 and 1937 by Robert Watson-Watt and his team working on an aerial defence system known initially as Radio Direction Finding, the name later changing to Radio Direction and Ranging then Radar. After a short stay at Orford Ness they moved the short distance to Bawdsey Manor where experiments continued.

The idea arose to design, build and set-up a chain of early warning systems around the coast of the British Isles in the late Thirties. The importance of this decision of early warning of air attack was considered vital, as at that time, all the country had was the Observer Corp and a concrete acoustic mirror sound locator next to Romney Marshes which only had a range of about 10 miles. Twenty stations along the south coast of England were operational just in time for the forthcoming air battles of 1940 and were located at specific locations so that their detection patterns overlapped with one another. Other criteria meant that no station was to be more than two miles from the coast, with masts as high as at least 200 feet and located on land at least fifty feet above the sea level. The transmitting towers were constructed of steel and were 300 to 350 feet high and were set in a line of usually four, the receiving aerials were constructed of wood and were 240 feet high and these four aerials were grouped together in the corner of the station. The sites also contained a number of smaller buildings which consisted of a transmitter and receiver block and offices where radar displays were situated plus accommodation for the personnel.

The operating principle of Chain Home (CH) was to keep the sky under surveillance by sending out pulses of energy or 'echoes' sent back to a receiver on the ground, the range of the aircraft being the precise measurement from the elapsed time between the pulse and the echo. This could be used to detect aircraft up to 100+ miles away and determine the height as well as the range and also the number of aircraft in a formation.

Chain Home Radar Station Locations

Radar Station	RAF Airfield Used
Tannach, Wick, Caithness	Wick, Highlands
Schoolhill, Porthlethen, Aberdeenshire	Peterhead, Grampian
Drone Hill, near Coldingham, Borders	Charterhall, Near Greenlaw, Borders
Stenigot, Louth, Lincolnshire	Manby, Louth, Lincolnshire
Swingate, Dover, Kent	Hawkinge, Near Folkestone, Kent
Rye, East Sussex	Hawkinge
Pevensey, East Sussex	Friston, Near Eastbourne, East Sussex
Poling, West Sussex	Ford and Tangmere, West Sussex
Southbourne, Dorset	Christchurch, Hants, now Dorset
Branscombe, Devon	Exeter, Devon
Downderry, Cornwall	Roborough, Plymouth Airport

Prominent People Mentioned in the ORB of 529 (Rota) Squadron

Group Captain John Ruskin Appleyard (Chaplain)
Air Marshal Sir Philip Babington AOC in C, Flying Training Command
Group Captain Jasper George Cardale SOA HQ 60 Group
Air Vice Marshal C. H. K. Edmonds AOA at HQ Flying Training Command
Air Commodore Harry Aitken Hewat PMO (Medical)
Air Vice Marshal W. E. Theak AOC No 60 (Signals) Group
Group Captain John Gerard Willsley Weston (Signals)

Advanced Landing Grounds in the ORB visited by 529 (Rota) Squadron

A84	Chièvres-Mons, Belgium
B17	Caen-Carpiquet, France
B56	Evere, Belgium
B61	Ghent-St Denis Westrem, Belgium
B91	Nimègue-Kluis (Nijmegen), Holland
B106	Enschede-Twente (Hengelo), Holland

Anti-Aircraft Guns

Calibrating the anti-aircraft (AA) guns was a similar exercise to calibrating radar stations, first a ground oscillator was sent up to obtain a signal usually with the help of a barrage balloon, then bearing and height readings were taken using radar and a theodolite after which the readings could then be adjusted accordingly. The operation would then involve an aircraft or autogiro flying round and round in circles above the site at varying different heights and distances to check everything was accurate.

The anti-aircraft radar set, once calibrated could then be used to send a short burst of high frequency radio waves at fixed intervals and when these found a target they would be bounced back onto the receiver. As the pulse left the transmitter a timing device was triggered in the receiver, this measured the time it took to reach the target and would then be returned back, this could then determine the distance of the plane.

When enemy planes had been detected by the radar, their location and bearing, range and elevation were fed automatically into either the Kerrison Predictor, built by the Singer Sewing machine company or the Vickers Predictor used on larger guns, these were mechanical computers. Then the information was sent to the guns which the operators could then train on the target, the computer would then work out where the plane would be when the shell got there, as long as the plane had not taken avoiding action.

An example of 529 Squadron work is when they were engaged in calibration flights during 1944 (see the operational records) along the East Coast of England using Ipswich airfield as a base for calibration work on guns defending the coast from V-1 attacks.

No. 60 (SIGNALS) GROUP

No.60 (Signals) Group was formed in March 1940 under the control of Fighter Command, their headquarters were situated at Oxenden House in Plantation Road, Leighton Buzzard in Buckinghamshire, under the command of Air Vice Marshal later Air Commodore W. E. Theak. They were responsible for all of the ground based radar and navigational aids in the country and worked closely with 529 Squadron whenever on detachment. The Group was split into various different Wings, (listed below) each responsible for their own radar station areas. The Communication Flight for the Group Headquarters had originally been based at Halton but moved to Wing airfield near Leighton Buzzard during late 1944 or early 1945. Airspeed Oxfords from 529 Squadron were frequent visitors to Wing airfield, mostly to collect officers and staff of the group.

70 (Signals) Wing, responsible for radar stations from Shetland to the Moray Firth.
72 (Signals) Wing, responsible for radar stations from Tees to the Firth of Forth, and later became responsible for Air Ministry Experimental Stations (AMES) including, ground radar stations and signals units in Great Britain and also units on the Continent.
75 (Signals) Wing, responsible for radar stations from the Thames to the Isle of Wight.
78 (Signals) Wing, responsible for radar stations in the Plymouth area.

'This plaque was erected by Leighton-Linslade Town Council on 23rd February 2000 to mark the 60th anniversary of the formation here No. 60 Signals Group, Fighter Command, Royal Air Force, the group responsible for Britain's radar defences in World War II'

In the words of the Commander-in-Chief Fighter Command,
"Without 60 Group and Radar the Battle of Britain, even the war itself, could not have been won"

The above monument is located outside Oxenden House, Leighton Buzzard.
Picture supplied by John Bernard Jones.

Cierva C30A (Avro Rota) Development

Avro Rota I DR624 'KX-L' (RTR Collection)

Juan de la Cierva was born in Spain in 1859, his interest in aviation began when he started to construct various gliders and aeroplanes in his youth. After an unsuccessful attempt at building a tri-motor bomber for the Spanish Government Cierva turned his attention to vertical flight, his idea was to create an aircraft that would be independent of speed for safety in flight. His idea was to have the wings rotate freely in flight by aerodynamic and not mechanical means. After many problems had been overcome due to stability and various other factors he successfully flew his first machine in January 1923. The structure of this first machine consisted of a conventional aeroplane type fuselage and tail and had an engine fitted for forward flight but with a rotor fixed above the fuselage.

The "Jumping" Autogiro

The "jumping" Autogiro, as it was some times known or the "direct take-off" machine, would rise vertically from the ground and could land without run. It can do this by virtue of energy which is stored in the rotating blades. The blades are set at an angle of zero lift and are spun up by the engine to a high rate of revolution, the engine is then de-clutched from the rotors and they immediately assume a lifting angle and cause the aircraft to rise upwards. A jump of ten feet or more could be achieved, and at the top of the jump the Autogiro is brought into level flight and is drawn forward by the airscrew. The autogiro is constructed of steel tube with the tail section built of wood and then covered overall in fabric.

Production

The Cierva C30 was put into production under license at the Avro works in Manchester in 1934 as the Avro 671 Rota I and about 100 machines were constructed most of them were built for commercial use and for private flying but the Air Ministry ordered ten for Army Co-operation work, and at the outbreak of the war in 1939 several of the privately owned machines were impressed into service with the RAF. Serial numbers of RAF machines ran from K4230-K4239, V1186-V1187, AP506-AP510, BV999, DR622-DR624, HM580-HM581. Two others K4296 and K4775 were used for test work.

Fifteen Avro Rotas were used by 529 (Rota) Squadron when they were based at Henley-on-Thames eleven of which were ex civilian machines, five of which survive today.

Surviving 529 (Rota) Squadron Autogiros

K4232

Built by Avro as build No.R3/CA.954 under licence at Newtown Heath, Manchester in 1934 and was taken on RAF charge on the 25th August and first entered service with the School of Army Co-operation Flight at Old Sarum, Wiltshire. On the 15th February 1936 it went to 2 Squadron at Hawkinge, Kent before moving to the Aeroplane & Armament Experimental Establishment at Martlesham Heath, Suffolk on the 21st August. It returned to the School of Army Co-operation Flight on the 4th October 1937. From the 5th September it went to No.26 Maintenance Unit, Cowley having flown 88 hours before going into storage at Hanworth and later Hamble and was struck off charge on the 6th May 1939. In May 1939 it was at Old Warden with the Warden Aviation and Engineering Co. and was offered for sale but not sold due to the outbreak of war. It was brought out of storage on the 1st July 1940 for use by No.5 Radio Maintenance Unit, Duxford. In September of that year it was re-named No.5 Radio Servicing Station. In February 1941 it became No.74 Wing, this then became No.1448 (Rota) Flight and a month later moved to Halton, Buckinghamshire. On the 10th October 1942 it suffered Category.B damage and was sent to Cunliffe-Owen at Eastleigh, Southampton for repair, returning to Halton on the 11th March 1943. The unit was renumbered as 529 (Rota) Squadron on the 15th June 1943. The Squadron then moved to Henley-on-Thames in August 1944. When the Squadron disbanded it went to 5 Maintenance Unit, Kemble for disposal. It was sold to the Cierva Autogiro Co. at Southampton, then sold on to Sweden for Rolf von Bahrs Co. in July 1946 where it was registered as SE-AZB. It stayed in Sweden until 11th June 1978 when it was purchased by the RAF Museum, Hendon. It arrived back in the UK on the SS Stellaria at Tilbury Docks. Restored at Cardington, Bedfordshire it went on display at Hendon in 1981. From August 1996 to January 1998 it was loaned to the Spanish Air Force in association with the Juan de la Cierva Foundation to act as a pattern for a flying replica, upon return it went back to Hendon for display.
Photo: K4232 at the RAF Museum, Hendon (DJP)

K4232 as SE-AZB in Sweden
(Swedish Aviation Historical Society)

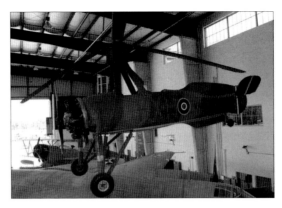

K4235

Built by Avro as build No.R3/CA/43 under licence at Newtown Heath, Manchester in 1934 and was taken on RAF charge on the 29th August and first entered service with the School of Army Co-operation Flight at Old Sarum, Wiltshire, in September. It was put into storage at No.26 Maintenance Unit, Cowley in March 1939 having completed 168 flying hours. In May 1939 it was at Old Warden with the Warden Aviation and Engineering Co. and was offered for sale but not sold due to the outbreak of war. It was brought out of storage in 1940 for the Autogiro Training Flight, this Flight was later absorbed into No. 5 Radio Maintenance Unit when it moved to Duxford in July 1940. In September of that year it was re-named No.5 Radio Servicing Station. In February 1941 it became No.74 Wing, this then became No.1448 (Rota) Flight and a month later moved to Halton, Buckinghamshire this unit was renumbered as 529 (Rota) Squadron in June 1943. On the 24th May 1944 it was damaged in a crash taking off from Ford and was sent to the Contractors by 49 MU for repair. The Squadron then moved to Henley-on-Thames in August 1944. When the Squadron disbanded it went to 5 Maintenance Unit, Kemble for disposal. Sold on the civilian market on 8th May 1946 to Fairey Aviation at White Waltham, being registered as G-AHMJ and used for design research for their Gyrodyne project. It was dismantled by 1947 and donated to the Hayes and Harlington Sea Cadets at Heston, before being acquired by the Shuttleworth Trust at Old Warden, Bedfordshire during 1954. Rebuilt possibly using parts from DR624/G-AHMI, K4239/G-AIOC and BV999/G-ACXW, it was later restored by Ken Hyde amongst others to taxying status until sold to Fantasy of Flight at Polk City, Florida USA in November 1998.

Photo: K4235 'KX-H' displayed at Fantasy of Flight, Polk City, Florida. (Peter Fitzmaurice Collection)

K4235 when owned by the Shuttleworth Trust
at Old Warden, Bedfordshire in 1994 (DJP)

DR624 as G-AHMI, parts of this autogiro are
said to have been used in the rebuild of K4235

AP506

Built by Avro as build No.715 under licence at Newtown Heath, Manchester in 1934. It was registered as G-ACWM on the 24th July. It was sold to Mr. Albert Batchelor on the 18th February 1935 and based at Ramsgate, Kent. During 1939 it went through a series of owners until being flown to Hendon during December for use by 24 Squadron for wireless calibration work. Impressed into the RAF as AP506 on the 1st June 1940 going No.5 Radio Servicing Station at Duxford. In February 1941 it was renamed No.74 Wing, this then became No.1448 (Rota) Flight and a month later moved to Halton, Buckinghamshire before being renumbered again as 529 (Rota) Squadron in June 1943. The Squadron then moved to Henley-on-Thames in August 1944. When the Squadron disbanded it went to 5 Maintenance Unit, Kemble for disposal. Sold on the civilian market in May 1946 it again became G-ACWM owned by Mr. H. R. Philip of Herne Bay. in 1953 it was acquired by a Mr. D. Butcher, his plan was to restore the machine with a new identity as G-AHMK however it was damaged in an arson attack and was destined to be stored in the rafters of his Tewkesbury garage. It was later stored at Staverton, Gloucestershire until it was rescued by Elfan ap Rees and put on display at Weston-Super-Mare.

Photo: AP506 in as found condition at The Helicopter Museum, Weston-Super-Mare. (DJP)

The frame of G-ACWM stacked against the hangar wall
at Staverton, Gloucestershire in May 1986 (Ken Tilley)

AP507

Built by Avro as build No.728 under licence at Newtown Heath, Manchester in 1934. It was registered as G-ACWP to a Mr. E. J. Jobling at Hanworth on the 16th November, and by October 1938 had been sold to Mr. Meikle and registered to the Autogiro Flying Club also at Hanworth during March 1939. It was impressed into the RAF during June 1940 as AP507 and was used initially by the Royal Aircraft Establishment at Farnborough and then transferred to the No.5 Radio Maintenance Unit when it moved to Duxford in July 1940. In September of that year it was re-named as No.5 Radio Servicing Station. Then in February 1941 it became No.74 Wing, this then became No.1448 (Rota) Flight and a month later moved to Halton, Buckinghamshire before being renumbered as 529 (Rota) Squadron in June 1943. From the 6th October to the 11th it was loaned to the Admiralty at Sydenham for trials with anti-submarine gear before returning to 529 Squadron. The Squadron then moved to Henley-on-Thames in August 1944. W/O Davidson in AP507 crashed on landing at Henley on a training flight on the 27th February 1945 is was repaired at the airfield, the pilot was unhurt. It was retired from service on the 18th May 1945 going to 5 Maintenance Unit, Kemble for disposal. It was sold to the Science Museum and moved to 76 Maintenance Unit, Wroughton for storage until being refurbished for display during 1961 by the apprentices at No.1 School of Technical Training at Halton. On the 10th July 1963 it was placed on display in the aviation gallery of the Science Museum.

Photo: AP507 'KX-P' displayed in the Science Museum, South Kensington, London. (DJP)

Genet Major radial piston engine on the Science Museum's Avro Rota. (DJP)

HM580

Built by Avro as build No.726 under licence at Newton Heath, Manchester in 1934 it was registered as G-ACUU on 26th June 1934 and used by Air Service Training at Hamble, Hampshire until 1938 and later put into store. It was impressed into the RAF on the 9th September 1942 as HM580 with No.1448 (Rota) Flight at Halton, Buckinghamshire before changing to 529 (Rota) Squadron in June 1943. On the 18th of October 1943 its career nearly ended when it crashed in bad weather returning to Thornaby in Yorkshire being flown by P/O Gillies, it was struck off charge although considered repairable. It was sent to Cunliffe-Owen at Eastleigh, Southampton and rebuilt by them by 24th January 1944 returning to 529 Squadron. The Squadron then moved to Henley-on-Thames in August 1944. On the 26th November 1945 it was sent to 5 Maintenance Unit, Kemble for disposal becoming the last Autogiro to fly with the RAF. Sold in 1946 and registered as G-AIXE to the Cierva Autogiro Co. at Southampton for overhaul, during which it was discovered to actually be G-ACUU to which it was restored to the register on the 3rd December 1946. In 1950 it was sold to Mr. Guy Spencer Baker who flew it from Elmdon, Birmingham until 1955 when it was stored, he then loaned to the Skyfame Museum at Staverton, Gloucestershire during the 1960's before it was relocated to Duxford during the 1970's where it is currently displayed as part of the Imperial War Museum collection.

Photo: HM580 'KX-K' displayed at the Imperial War Museum, Duxford. (DJP)

HM580 seen as G-ACUU at the Skyfame Museum at Staverton, Gloucestershire in a red and grey colour scheme.

HM580 seen in an earlier paint scheme representing its impressment colours of No.1448 (Rota) Flight. (DJP)

Non-Surviving aircraft of 529 (Rota) Squadron after 1945

K4233   sold 7-5-1946 Registered as G-AHXI 29-6-1946 Sold to Belgium as OO-ADK 5-7-1948

Avro 671 Rota G-AIOC
at Hereford racecourse in 1947.
(W/Cdr Mike Edwards via Dave Welch)

K4239   Registered as G-AIOC 16-10-1946 and damaged beyond repair at Elstree 10-7-1949

Avro 671 Rota G-ACWO

V1187   ex G-ACWO to Southern Aircraft (Gatwick) sold to Sweden for spares use 1948

Avro 671 Rota SE-AZA
(Swedish Aviation Historical Society)

AP509   ex G-ACWS sold to the Cierva Autogiro Co Ltd registered as G-AHUC 11-6-1946,
sold to Sweden 17-7-1946 and registered as SE-AZA 17-9-1946 to Rolf Van Bahr
of Stockholm, then sold onto the Örebro Flying Club 11-11-1949 before they sold it to
H. Liljedahl, at Gällivare 9-1-1951 before finally being sold to G. Forsberg, A. Åslund,
and E. Olsson at Sandviken it was cancelled from the register on 21-2-1958

AP510   ex G-ACYE restored as G-ACYE 4-12-1946 and withdrawn from use by 4-1947

BV999   ex G-ACXW to Fairey Aviation Co, White Waltham restored as G-ACXW 8-5-1946
to an unidentified Air Training Corps Unit at Twickenham in 1951 with parts later
believed used by the Shuttleworth Trust in the rebuild of K4235

DR622   ex G-ACYH registered as G-AHRP 28-5-1946 withdrawn from use at White Waltham
         24-7-1948 and later to Eastleigh 27-8-1949

Avro 671 Rota G-ACWH
(Charles Holland Collection via Ken Tilley)

DR623   ex G-ACWH sold to Cierva Autogiro Co Ltd and registered as G-AHLE 26-4-1946
         withdrawn from use at Eastleigh 6-1947 to 1440 Air Training Corps Unit at Shoreham
         and broken up 2-1952, its engine being donated to the RAF Museum.

Avro 671 Rota G-ACWF

Avro 671 Rota DR624
at Aldenham airfield (RTR Collection)

DR624   ex G-ACWF, Displayed at the ATA Pageant at White Waltham 29th September 1945
         as DR624. Sold to the Fairey Aviation Co, White Waltham 4-1946 and registered as
         G-AHMI 8-5-1946, dismantled by June 1947 and donated to the Shuttleworth Trust
         parts of DR624 are said to have been used in the rebuild of K4235.

HM581   ex G-ACUI sold to Essex Aero Ltd and registered as G-AHTZ 11-6-1946 and crashed
         at Elmdon, Birmingham 4-3-1958

Avro 671 Rota G-ACUI

Avro 671 Rota G-AHTZ

de Havilland Tiger Moth G-AHLD

de Havilland Tiger Moth

T6864   sold as G-AHLD 26th April 1946, then sold to New Zealand as ZK-AUY, 21st July 1950
          Crashed near Raetihi, New Zealand 12th January 1953.

Airspeed Oxford

T1210   allocated to 527 Squadron and eventually sold as scrap 18th March 1949.

X7238   allocated to 519 Squadron and struck off charge 7th August 1947

de Havilland Hornet Moth

W5830   ex G-ADKE to de Havilland at Witney, Oxfordshire for major inspection 9th April 1945
          but struck off charge during inspection 13th July 1945.

X9310   ex G-ADMR to de Havilland at Witney, Oxfordshire for major inspection 1st May 1945
          but struck off charge during inspection 16th July 1945.

529 (Rota) Squadron de Havilland Hornet Moths after 1945

W5749 seen as G-ADKK
at The Great Vintage Flying Weekend
RAF Hullavington 21st May 2005
owned by R. M. & D. R. Lee. (DJP)

W5750 seen as G-ADKL
at Luton, Bedfordshire 23rd June 1963
current on the UK civil register 2010.
(Peter Fitzmaurice Collection)

W5754 seen as G-ADKW
Withdrawn from use in 1948.
(Charles Holland Collection via Ken Tilley)

W5777 seen as G-AEWY
at White Waltham, Berkshire in the 1950's
when owned by West London Aero Services
it crashed at Barton 18th April 1964.
(©Tom Pharo via Air Britain)

W5779 seen as G-AFDT
Crashed at Dinas Powis near Penarth 1951.
(Charles Holland Collection via Ken Tilley)

W9383 seen as G-AEKY
Withdrawn from use at Croydon 1953.
(Charles Holland Collection via Ken Tilley)

W9389 seen as VH-AMJ ex G-ADMJ
at Moorabbin, Victoria, Australia in 1956
currently registered as VH-AFJ.
(Photo by Ed Coates)

AV952 seen as G-ADSK
at Stapleford, Essex in 1961 when owned by
Patrick Lyons, it is currently in New Zealand.
(Peter Fitzmaurice Collection)

THE OLD HATCH GATE

The Old Hatch Gate Public House at Cockpole Green was used by the 529 Squadron NCO's when they first arrived at the airfield as their Mess before supplies arrived from RAF Shinfield Park in Reading. The landlord George Denton (pictured) treated them very courteously and was later rewarded for his efforts when he was presented with a wooden propeller and plaque at the end of 1945 or beginning of 1946 when the Squadron finally left the area. This hung on the wall over the bar for many years after the war. The Dentons eventually left and the pub is now a private house. With thanks to Tony Verey.
(Photo supplied by Brakspears Pub Company)

A GIFT FROM 529 (ROTA) SQUADRON

The propeller and wooden plaque presented by 529 (Rota) Squadron to George Denton, landlord of The Old Hatch Gate. The inscription, in red and black reads, 'For Auld Lang Syne' RAF 529 Rota Squadron 1944-46. With thanks to Len Denton (Photographs supplied by Len Denton)

Cierva W.9

Cierva W.9 PX203. (V. Flintham Collection)

Designed by G. & J. Weir Ltd and built under specification E.16/43. This was a two-seat experimental all-metal helicopter design powered by a 205 h.p. de Havilland Gipsy Six inline piston engine which drove a three-bladed rotor. What was unusual about the design was that instead of a tail rotor a jet thrust arrangement was installed, this consisted of an opening situated on the port side of the tail boom, the air from a fan which was used to cool the engine was ducted through the fuselage then heated by the exhaust gases and then through the opening, two horizontal shutters controlled the air-flow. Another important part of the design was the hydraulically powered shaft-driven tilting rotor hub with rotational speed variation to give automatic collective pitch control. One W.9 was built at Hanworth serial number PX203 during 1944 and the machine built and ground-tested during October 1944. Tethered runs were carried out on a small piece of ground outside the factory building at Thames Ditton, Surrey in early 1945 and during early engine runs it was damaged, this being caused by the controls being manual and the tilting-hub of the rotors becoming unmanageable. The W.9 was rebuilt and power controls were installed. Tests continued and the machine moved to the airfield at Henley-on-Thames, probably using the site vacated by the M.A.P. Spitfire hangars. Here S/L Alan Marsh did some tethered flights of no more than a few feet off the ground, the results of which turned out to be not very encouraging. Alterations were made back at Thames Ditton to the flying controls and the anti-torque system and the rear fuselage altered to allow air to flow more freely to the tail nozzle. A vertical tail fin was added later presumably to aid stability. Test flying continued at Eastleigh Airport, Southampton from 1946 again with Alan Marsh doing the tests who now became the Chief Test Pilot on the W.9. The Company had taken over the former Cunliffe-Owen factory at Southampton. Improvements were carried out to the design and eventually it achieved a modest performance. It was publicly unveiled at the Air League Air Pageant at Southampton on the 22nd June 1946 and later on in the year it went on to perform at the Society of British Aircraft Manufacturers (SBAC) show at Radlett, Hertfordshire with demonstrations of hovering and backward flying. By this time panels had been removed from the side framework. A second W.9 PX207 was due to be built but when PX203 was damaged beyond repair in 1946 after it had rolled over due to duel controls being fitted on the orders of the Air Ministry. The project came to an end after the accident although according to Jacob Shapiro the Chief Technical Officer for the design it did produce some very valuable lessons in helicopter design and techniques.

Man Pick-up Installation Trials

Malcolm Aviation (ML Aviation) based at White Waltham devised the 'Man Pick-up Installation'. It was developed as a means of snatching agents out of occupied Europe without having to risk aircraft having to land. Two poles would be positioned about 25 feet apart, the person to be 'lifted' would sit on the ground between the poles facing the incoming aircraft. Attached to his back, in the form of a harness, would be a looped cable, the top of which would be strung across the two poles. The aircraft would pay out a highly elastic nylon cable to which was attached a hook, a winch in the aircraft would then winch in the occupant. Tests were carried out at White Waltham with a Armstrong-Whitworth Whitley and a Handley-Page Halifax. Trials were also carried out at Upper Culham Farm airfield by the Royal Aircraft Establishment for a short time during the summer of 1945 with an Avro Anson X NK234 flown by W. J. Carn over from Farnborough every day. Using a dummy person in place of a real human, the trials did have draw-backs apparently as the stuffing kept falling out of the dummy, although the tests were successful enough to perfect the technique. Further tests were carried out at Farnborough with a live volunteer, the first and possibly the last live volunteer to be picked up in this way was Wing Commander Roland Winfield, a doctor at the RAF Institute of Aviation Medicine at Farnborough, Hampshire. He would sit on the ground in a foetal position ready to be 'snatched,' once up in the air he would detach himself from the hook and descend by parachute back to terra-ferma. If the project had been carried further it was the intention to winch the person into the aeroplane. The project was never developed beyond the testing stage.

A test underway with a dummy about to be 'snatched.'
from between the two poles by a Handley-Page Halifax at White Waltham
(ML Aviation Archive, Museum of Berkshire Aviation)

Airfield Accidents, Incidents and Visiting Aircraft

On the 23rd October 1941 P/O W. Retingers of 308 Squadron at Northolt was on a night training flight when his radio failed, he landed at Henley which must have been lit up for night training by 8 EFTS at the time and his Spitfire V, possibly W3798 was slightly damaged.

On the 24th February 1943 at 15.30 pm Vickers Wellington III BJ798 'AL-E' of 429 Squadron, from East Moor in Yorkshire flown by F/O G. Fox, mistook Henley airfield for White Waltham and force-landed on the airfield, it ending up skidding on the wet grass and crossing Upper Culham Lane at the end of the runway before coming to rest in a field, resulting in the fuselage breaking in half.

A de Havilland Tiger Moth had taken off from the airfield only to struggle to get airborne, it clipped some trees and somehow managed to turn itself back around facing the opposite direction and deposit itself on the roof of Sir Edwin Speed's house in Upper Culham Lane. The undercarriage went through the roof tiles and this stopped the aircraft in it's tracks, luckily without injury to the pilot. The aircraft was taken to pieces in situ in a slightly damaged state.

One Christmas early in the war a de Havilland Mosquito landed and parked up on the airfield next to the Upper Culham Lane, it caused much excitement to the local lads who cycled to the airfield to see it through the wire fence. The visit was apparently a social one and could well have been connected with the 13 Elementary Flying Training School which was run by the de Havilland company. One of the lads who joined the Air Cadets soon after, when asked during an aircraft recognition test what the aircraft was, surprised his superiors by exclaiming it as a Mosquito, which at the time hadn't even entered service with the RAF.

A bomber aircraft possibly an Armstrong-Whitworth Whitley on a night flight is said to have force-landed at Henley when night-flying was taking place by one of the training units here, it force-landed on the airfield after it's undercarriage collapsed, it was dismantled and taken away either as scrap or for use as a maintenance airframe. It is not known when the accident happened.

A Hawker Tempest (possibly a prototype mark II) and probably on a test flight from nearby Langley suffered engine failure at altitude and ended up having to force-land on the airfield. The aircraft is reported as being taken away after being covered up by a tarpaulin.

An incident involving three P-47s trying to land at Henley ended up with one of them stuck in the ballast gravel at the end of the runway, this would have been used for filling in holes if the field suffered any bomb damage, the other two pilots seeing this decided not to land. The P-47 having been recovered from it's predicament had to have it's underwing fuel tanks removed to reduce weight but eventually managed to take off again.

A Squadron of Spitfires are said to have landed here short of fuel, and a Short Stirling apparently once did some touch and go training here.

Air Transport Auxiliary (ATA) visits

Aircraft from the ATA would have been frequent visitors to Henley during the time that Vickers were here assembling Spitfires between May 1941 and December 1942 as after test-flights they needed ferrying, usually to a Maintenance Unit. The following are known visits by the ATA.

Hugh Bergel a ATA pilot flew a de Havilland Puss Moth into Henley on 5th June 1941 from Pershore, Worcestershire with one passenger aboard.
Stuart Franklin Updike an American ATA pilot flew a Fairchild Argus taxi aircraft into Henley at night on 4th April 1942, he managed to land by using the planes landing lights and his passenger shining a torch on the compass.

AIRFIELD BUILDINGS

The majority of the buildings on the airfield were of pre-fabricated construction designed for speed of construction and most of the huts for accommodation were of timber construction or more elaborate Laing hutting, others were of temporary brick construction. Brick buildings were designed to have a life span of ten years and were built of single brick, without a cavity wall. Outside the brickwork was rendered with cement whilst inside the walls were painted in various colours. The buildings had concrete floors. Wooden huts were assembled using timber-framed sections, these sections bolted together to form any length. The timber framed panels were covered on the outside with 3/4 inch weather boarding with the walls inside lined with plasterboard and with standard metal windows. Roofs were timber trussed and panelled and covered externally with corrugated asbestos or timber then felted, the floors to were made of timber. The Laing hut consisted of standard prefabricated lightweight timber wall sections bolted together. Nissen huts consisted of lengths of six feet wide curved corrugated iron sheets fixed to a steel frame and had a concrete floor. Corrugated steel sheets were laid horizontally on the inside and on the outside was corrugated iron sheeting. Wooden or brick ends each with two windows and a door frame they could be assembled quickly and the arched shape made it very strong.

Airmens Drying Rooms (Nos.9 & 10)
It was essential for flying clothing to be bone dry and this building contained the drying facilities. On the end of the building was the boiler room to provide the necessary heating for drying. The drying room was equipped with hanging rails on which to dry the clothing.

Dope Store (No.34)
This building was used to store the dope. Dope was a highly flammable liquid and needed careful storage.

Stand-By-Set House (No.28)
This building held the standby generator equipment for use if the main electrical supply failed.

Works Services Building (No.27)
This was used as a stores and workshop and held general equipment such as ladders, tools, etc.

NAAFI (No.1)
The NAAFI was created during 1921 to provide welfare and amenities for servicemen.
It was non profit making but sold goods like cigarettes to servicemen, as well as providing the tea.

Robins Hangar (No.101)
This was a design by the Air Ministry and could house two Spitfires at a time, known as the Robins Type 'B' these were manufactured by R.B & Co. and Dawnays.
Dimensions are 44 feet wide a door height of 14 feet and a length of 75 feet.

Compass Platform (Nos.36 & 38)
The compass platform was used to 'swing' or set the aircraft's compass. The platform was constructed as a concrete hard standing but it had a well in the centre and a circular wooden platform covering the top. A set of wheels ran in the well and enabled the platform to act as a turntable. The aircraft sat on top of the turntable and was turned to the compass points, north, east, south, and west and the aircraft's compass was checked for the correct reading and adjusted accordingly.

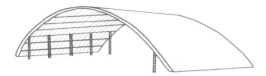

Blister Hangar (Nos.14, 15 & 29, 30)
Designed by W C Inman and G R Dawbarn, these were constructed by C Miskins and Sons. The original design called for a timber curved-arch covered by steel sheeting, these were known as Standard, two Blisters joined together made a Double Standard. Some had canvas curtains over the ends to offer some form of protection from the weather. Dimensions are a 25 feet long with a 45 foot span and a height of 14 feet, no foundations were used, as the load was spread evenly and being flexible enough to stand on uneven ground.

Airfield and Local Area Defences

The local Home Guard in Wargrave who started out as part of the Twyford Platoon in 1940 was re-organised during 1941 and separate platoons were organised around the area. Duties of the Home Guard included assisting in protecting the airfields of White Waltham and also Upper Culham Farm, keeping a watching brief on possible landing grounds and also managing road blocks in the case of an enemy attack. Anti-Aircraft guns were situated at nearby Hennerton and used during the Battle of Britain. The airfield itself had three known Cantilever Mushroom pillboxes situated around the outside perimeters, these are about 20 feet in diameter and sunken into the ground and made from brick with a concrete top, they had a metal rail running around the inside to which would have been attached a gun. They would have been used had the airfield been a target for German paratroopers. There is one which still survives the others having been destroyed or dug up.

A Cantilever Mushroom-Pillbox designed by F C Construction Co Ltd which gave a 360° view. This is the only remaining evidence of wartime activity, and is situated on the south boundary of the airfield at layout location 39. (DJP)

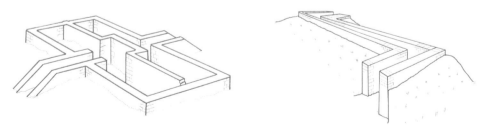

Blast shelters made of brick and usually situated near the technical area, so that taking shelter could if necessary be left until the last minute.

AIRFIELD LAYOUT

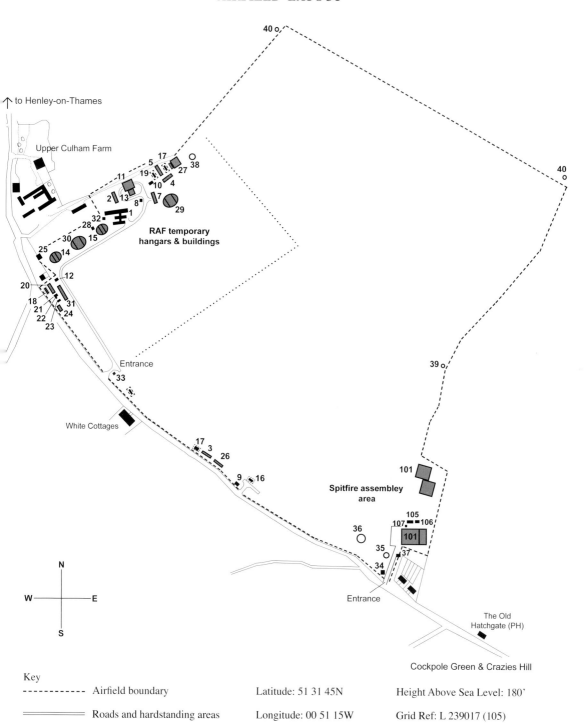

to Henley-on-Thames

Upper Culham Farm

40

40

RAF temporary
hangars & buildings

17
5
11
19
10
4
27
38
2
13
8
7
1
32
28
30
15
25
14
29

12
20
18
21
31
22
24
23

Entrance

33

White Cottages

17
3
26

9
16

39

Spitfire assembley
area

101

105
107   106
101

36

35
37
34

Entrance

The Old
Hatchgate (PH)

Cockpole Green & Crazies Hill

N
W   E
S

Key

--------- Airfield boundary

========= Roads and hardstanding areas

Landing area: Grass 700-800 yds SSW-NNE
recommended extension to 1600 yds entails demolition of a cottage

Copied from No.11 Works Area Drawing No. HEN/1586/44.

Latitude: 51 31 45N

Longitude: 00 51 15W

Height Above Sea Level: 180'

Grid Ref: L 239017 (105)

O.S. Ref: SU 795824

·········· Area later used as a polo field

AIRFIELD BUILDINGS

No.	BUILDING	CONSTRUCTION	Drawing No.
1.	DINING ROOM, SGTS. MESS, & N.A.A.F.I.	TIMBER	1032/41
2.	A.M's & SGTS, QUARTERS	TIMBER	"
3.	OFFICERS QUARTERS	TIMBER	"
4.	AIRMENS BARRACKS	TIMBER	"
5.	" "	TIMBER	"
6.	" (FLOOR BASE ONLY)	TIMBER	
7.	OFFICERS, SGTS & A.M's ABLUTIONS	TEMPORARY BRICK	1033/41
8.	OFFICERS, SGTS & A.M's LATRINES	TEMPORARY BRICK	"
9.	A.M's DRYING ROOM & LATRINES	TEMPORARY BRICK	"
10.	A.M's DRYING ROOM & E.T. ROOM	TEMPORARY BRICK	"
11.	FUEL COMPOUND		
12.	CIVILIAN REST ROOM	TEMPORARY BRICK	9794/41
13.	FIRE TANK		TP/4172/41
14.	BLISTER HANGAR (STANDARD TYPE)	TIMBER	12494/41
15.	" " " "	TIMBER	"
16.	PETROL INSTALLATION 4000 GAL. TANK		
17.	AIR RAID SHELTER (50 MAN TYPE) x 2	PERMANENT BRICK	
18.	BLAST SHELTER (50 MAN)	PERMANENT BRICK	TP/4038/41
19.	" " (25 MAN)	PERMANENT BRICK	"
20.	A.M's QUARTERS & STORES (54' 9" x 16' 8")	TIMBER	
21.	A.M's QUARTERS (22' 3" x 12' 6")	TIMBER	
22.	STORE (10' 2" x 6' 3")	TEMPORARY BRICK	
23.	M.T. & DISCIPLINARY OFFICE (22' 3" x 12' 6")	TIMBER	
24.	M.I. CRASH ROOM & EQUIPMENT STORE	NISSEN	
25.	LATRINE	TIMBER	
26.	OFFICERS MESS (LAING HUTTING)		
27.	WORKS SERVICES BUILDING	NISSEN	7393/41
28.	STAND-BY-SET HOUSE	TEMPORARY BRICK	10952/40
29.	BLISTER HANGAR (DOUBLE STANDARD TYPE)	TIMBER	12494/41
30.	" " " " "	TIMBER	"
31.	WATCH OFFICE & H.Q. OFFICE	NISSEN	S3/TP/58/42
32.	W.A.A.F. CLOSET (6' 3" x 3' 8")	TEMPORARY BRICK	
33.	GUARD HUT (16' x 11' 6")	TIMBER	
34.	DOPE STORE	PERMANENT BRICK	
35.	FIRE TANK 20,000 GALLON (34' diameter)	STEEL	
36.	COMPASS PLATFORM (37' 6" diameter)		
37.	STORE (16' x 14' 6 ")	CORRUGATED IRON	
38.	COMPASS PLATFORM (32' 0" diameter)		
39.	CANTILEVER PILLBOX	BRICK & CONCRETE	
40.	(Approximate locations of other Cantilever pillboxes)		

Ministry of Aircraft Production Buildings loaned to the Air Ministry

101.	ROBINS HANGARS, WORKSHOPS & OFFICES		
105.	AIR RAID SHELTER	PERMANENT BRICK	
106.	SEWAGE INSTALLATION (SEPTIC TANK)		
107.	PETROL INSTALLATION (3,000) DISUSED		

Most buildings were given a Air Ministry Works number or Drawing number, they usually consist of four to five numbers with a suffix indicating the year of design.

AFTER THE WAR

After the Second World War had ended and 529 (Rota) Squadron had disbanded they finally left the site in late 1945 or early 1946, the RAF sold off the contents of the airfield including some Nissen hut buildings and lorries and equipment and by 1947 the blister hangars and two of the Robins hangars appear to have gone, the concrete perimeter road was later dug up. Some of the huts were used for temporary housing for a short time and most of the other brick buildings were demolished although some survived into the 1960's. One of the Spitfire production hangars now known as Warren Works was taken over in early 1949 by Hunter-Penrose Ltd, who manufactured items of printing equipment, this building was later taken over by Toga Toy Manufacturing Ltd but was destroyed by fire on the 30th July 1966. New buildings were erected and continued to be used by Toga and by Anglocentrop Furniture, a mail-order company. Further development of the site has now seen housing replace these buildings during the early 1990's. Part of the northern area of the airfield became the Henley Polo Club from May 1947 for use by the Household Brigade of Guards because their ground at Smiths Lawn, Windsor had not been released by the Ministry of Agriculture from crop growing. Dignitaries such as Lord Mountbatten, Prince Philip, Lord Cowdrey and Lord David's Friar Park team, Indian Rajah's including the Maharajah of Jaipore and other notable players of the time played there. They used the former Mess and NAAFI buildings as stables. It is possible that some of the players used light aircraft when arriving for the matches.

Upper Culham Farm and the area where the RAF hangars and buildings used to be is now part of a small business park and the airfield has reverted back to agriculture and apart from a surviving cantilever-pillbox gun emplacement nothing remains of this former airfield.

The Henley Model Club

Members of Henley Model Club during 1953, Back Row from left: Phil Pengilley, Derek Wilkinson,
John Sargeant, Don Palmer, Roy Cooke, John Arlett, Bruce Garrett
Middle Row: Michael Bird, Dave Painter, Tony Cooke, Jim Waldron, Herbert Dory
Front Row: Terry Trendall, Phil Buckett

Flying did continue at the airfield albeit on a slightly smaller scale as the site was sometimes used by members of the local Henley Model Club for testing their latest creations, formed in 1946-7 and sponsored by Bill Aston who ran Astons Toy and Model shop in Hart Street. Their first flying field was at Badgemore Park before moving onto Upper Culham Farm. On one occasion a club member, Derek Wilkinson was testing his 'Fugitive' model glider when it flew away and disappeared only to find out later that it had landed on one of the runways during the construction of Heathrow airport. The club later gained permission from James Martin, of Martin-Baker Ltd the manufacturer of ejection seats, to use Chalgrove airfield in Oxfordshire, here they could make use of the mile long runway.

Hunter-Penrose Ltd

This company who had taken over one of the former Spitfire hangars on the airfield in early 1949, had in wartime been kept busy manufacturing equipment for the Ministry of Supply, items such as enlargers for the Air Force, as well as special cameras for use on top secret projects for photographing enemy manoeuvres over the channel. After the war the company was producing arc lamps and cameras many of which were shipped abroad, they were also allowed with Government control to import from America Vandercook proof presses and it is said that at the time every engraving house in the country had one of these machines. Other items made at the factory included slitting machines, cylinder proof presses, step and repeat, Deffa presses and also ruled glass screens.

The fire-gutted remains of the Toga Manufacturing Company hangar after a fire which broke out during Saturday the 30th July 1966, fire appliances from eight fire brigades attended the blaze.
(Henley Standard)

EMERGENCY AT COCKPOLE GREEN

"Operation Greenfly"

On Sunday the 15th April 1973 "Operation Greenfly" took place on land belonging to Mr. Jack Pring at Goulders Farm, Cockpole Green. The site just south of the former airfield was used for a simulated training exercise by the emergency services and recreated a situation if an aircraft had crashed taking off from Heathrow Airport. Local Police Cadets were used to play the corpses and members of the Casualty Union were made up as injured people, they lay scattered amongst the fuselage parts of a Armstrong-Whitworth Argosy transport aircraft, brought in by lorry to play the part of the actual aircraft which was supposed to have crashed on a London - Paris bound flight at 8.30 a.m. that morning. The idea of the exercise being to test the local Berkshire, Buckinghamshire and Oxfordshire emergency services, Cockpole Green was chosen for its central location and it is believed the site here or the old airfield site would have been an actual emergency crash-landing site for Heathrow if the situation arose, being a fairly large flat field not far from the flight path. A small fake fire had been lit in the aircraft's fuselage, which was soon extinguished and the ambulance brigade set up a casualty centre, taking the injured to ambulances which then took them to local hospitals in nearby Reading, they too were taking part in the exercise.

The photographs below by Nigel Dawe from the early 1990's show the site of the former Spitfire production area before it was redeveloped for housing as Ashley Hill Place.

Former site of one of the Spitfire production hangars when used by Toga Manufacturing Ltd, this building replaced the old hangar burnt down in 1966. (Nigel Dawe) Airfield layout location 101.

Air-raid shelter at the Spitfire production site. (Nigel Dawe) Airfield layout location 105.

This building is listed as a Dope Store but as it is situated near the entrance to the former Spitfire production hangars it could also be a Pill-box or Guard Hut. (Nigel Dawe) Airfield layout location 34.

Corrugated Iron Store Shed on the site of the former Spitfire
production area. (Nigel Dawe) Airfield layout location 37.

A Steel 20,000 Gallon Fire Tank by the former Spitfire
production area of the airfield. (Nigel Dawe)
Airfield layout location 35.

Entrance to the former Spitfire production hangars, when used by Toga Manufacturing
and Anglocentrop Ltd, now it is the entrance to Ashley Hill Place (Nigel Dawe)

A view showing the former airfield taken in 1983, with the site of the former Spitfire production hangars in the foreground, when used by Toga and Anglocentrop Furniture Ltd. and Upper Culham Lane running north towards Upper Culham Farm. (Ken Fostekew)

Ashley Hill Place, once the entrance to the Spitfire production site as it appears in 2010 (DJP)

A view across the airfield looking south-east towards Ashley Hill Place the former site of the Spitfire production hangars and workshops, with Upper Culham Lane on the right. (DJP)

View from the Henley to Maidenhead road looking across to the former RAF side of the airfield with the White Cottages on the left and Upper Culham Farm behind the trees on the right (DJP)

RAF Benson

Opened in February 1939 as a bomber base for Fairey Battle aircraft although they did not stay long as they left for France in September for the start of the 'Phoney War,' though some Battles still remained at the station. The airfield was chosen as the site for the Kings Flight and from the middle of September 1939 until February 1941 various aircraft were operated from here. During April 1940 12 Operational Training Unit (OTU) was set up here as a light bomber training unit again using the Fairey Battle although by the summer of that year it had re-equipped with the Vickers Wellington. The OTU was to stay until August 1941 when it moved to Chipping Warden. The next part of Benson's history is probably it's most famous because of the arrival in December 1940 of 1 Photographic Reconnaissance Unit (PRU) from it's then base of Heston. Here the PRU flew many different types of aircraft, the most famous being the Spitfire and Mosquito although they also operated Bristol Blenheims, Lockheed Hudsons and Martin Maryland's on photographic missions into occupied Europe for both Bomber Command and also Coastal Command, and the airfield was transferred to a Coastal Command Group station in August 1941. The connection with both Medmenham and also Phyllis Court is noted over the next two pages. It was in May 1942 that the airfield was upgraded with hard runways and all flying stopped here with everything moving to nearby Mount Farm. In October 1942 the PRU was reformed into four individual Squadrons 541, 542 and 543 with Spitfires and 544 with mostly the twin engined types. PRU operations continued here right up until the end of the war although by then it's role had changed from one of war to peacetime as Europe went about rebuilding itself. The post war years continued on the PR theme when 8 OTU later redesignated 237 Operational Conversion Unit (OCU) which were training units, and with the arrival of the Meteor and later the Canberra brought the PR era into the jet age. PR operations came to an end in March 1953 and Benson was transferred to Transport Command. During the sixties and seventies Benson was dominated by Argosy and Andover transport aircraft and the Royal Flight returned this time as the Queens Flight, until they relocated to Northolt in 1995. Helicopters are now the dominant type based here with both Merlin and Puma frequently active on training and operational flights. Benson has been and still is a very important RAF base and has certainly led a varied life.

A Scene in the Photographic Plotting Room in the Headquarters building at Benson in 1949
Jim Waldron is sitting at the head of the table next to the head of the department Pilot Officer Gibb (standing). Photographs were plotted individually on Ordnance Survey Maps 1 inch to mile (1/63360) maps (With thanks to Jim Waldron)

RAF Medmenham

It was during 1941 that the Photographic Interpretation Unit (PIU) moved from Wembley to Danesfield House, it get's it's name from a camp that was set up here by the Danish when they pillaged their way along the Thames between the eighth and tenth centuries. Situated overlooking the Thames between Henley and Marlow, the RAF base took its name from the nearby village of Medmenham.

Photographic interpretation carried out over the years here led appropriately to many photographs being taken by the Spitfire PR.IV aircraft built just across the river at Henley and flown from RAF Benson. Photographic missions were often at high altitude between 30,000ft and 38,000ft producing what were known as 'verticals' pictures that overlapped each other making up a mosaic although some were required to be at low level known as 'horizontals'. As soon as an aircraft had landed back at Benson the photographs would be developed and processed in buildings in the grounds of The Old Mansion at Ewelme, then from estimations the developed photographs could have the positions plotted, this was known as the 'first phase'. The 'second phase' was for the film to sent over to Danesfield House for interpretation after which a report would be sent to the Air Ministry. Much of the work was carried out by WAAF interpreters, these included the daughter of Sir Winston Churchill, Sarah Oliver and also Constance Babington-Smith amongst others. Photographs taken over the areas where the Germans had developed the Messerschmitt 163 'Komet, a liquid fuelled fighter, at Peenemunde were to prove beyond doubt that these were the sites where the dreaded V-1 and V-2 rockets were also being constructed during December 1942, and also the launch sites in northern France. Other work carried out here involved analyzing many photographs of the African landings, the Dambusters raid of May 1943, as well as the D-Day landings amongst many others.

Also based at Danesfield was V-Section of the Central Interpretation Unit (CIU) which established itself in the basement of the house. Here three dimensional models were constructed using photographs supplied by the PIU from which models of targets could be constructed, including the Bruneval radio location site. The unit moved to Phyllis Court in the summer of 1942 when the Americans joined the war and they combined with the CIU to make an allied model making group. The unit moved back to Danesfield during mid 1943. Models were prepared for air attacks on the dams at Eder, Sorpe, Mohne, for the Dambusters raid, indeed the models seen in the film the Dambusters are the actual models made for the attacks. Other models made were for raids on the ball-bearing works at Schweinfurt, the viaducts at Bielefeld and Neuenbecke, oil refineries at Ploesti, the ship lift at Magdeburg, and many others, plus various targets for South East Asia Command. Later on the unit supplied models of the experimental V-weapon sites at Peenemunde and various other launching sites. The unit was disbanded during 1944 after the Americans moved abroad to be closer to actual operations. This is just a small part of the history of this important location, and the whole story could fill a book itself. Today Danesfield House is a luxury hotel although there are photographic reminders of it's past history, but all of the site occupied by the various other huts and buildings has now been re-developed.

Phyllis Court

Situated on the banks of the river Thames at Henley-on-Thames is Phyllis Court a regency country house used as a private club, on the outbreak of war the ballroom here was taken over by the Ministry of Supply, which was used for the repair of optical instruments. When the Air Ministry moved into Danesfield House at nearby Medmenham, Phyllis Court was taken over as the mess for the WAAF officers who were only to happy to make use of the tranquil surroundings by the river, until they rather reluctantly had to move to rather more austere accommodation during 1942.

From mid 1942 an American Engineer Model-Making Detachment was set up here and joined forces with the RAF Central Interpretation Unit which relocated here from nearby Danesfield House at Medmenham although the personnel remained at Danesfield and were transported here by road each day. The unit eventually moved back to Danesfield in 1943 due to an increase in demand for model-making.

Stationed here later in the war, the location known as United States Army Air Force Station 494, were Detachment 0, and Detachment X, of the 93rd Station Complement Squadron Reinforcement Depot (SCSRD) United States Strategic Air Forces in Europe (USSTAFE), which was used for the rest and recreation of American aircrew, although this is not connected with the airfield itself but due to it's close proximity it is possible that aircraft of the United States Air Force may have made use of it. Also stationed at nearby Remenham, in tented accommodation, known as United States Army Air Force Station 925, from 12th January 1944 before moving to Newcastle in May, were the 573rd Signal Aircraft Warning Battalion, of XIX Air Support Command. This was a mobile radar unit who were later involved in the D-Day landings at Utah beach near Normandy. Again it is unclear wether they made any use of the airfield at Henley during their time here. Three Douglas C-47 Dakota transport aircraft were seen by a local working on farmland at the time, as visiting the airfield, and are most likely to have been connected with one of the nearby American camps of which there were many in the surrounding area, including a detachment of Eighth Army veterans, three battalions of American Combat Engineers and a Tank Engineering Battalion. Station 54a at Fawley Court, was a signals section for training agents/spies as wireless operators for the S.O.E.

Douglas C-47 Dakota USAAF transport aircraft. (DJP)

Local Wartime Accidents and Incidents

Supermarine Spitfire IIb P8725 'WX-B' of 302 Squadron RAF Heston, the pilot lost control during a formation training flight and the aircraft spun into the ground at Broadplatt Wood, Fairmile, Henley-on-Thames 29th May 1942 Flying Officer Alexander Godlewski died in the accident. **1**

Vickers Wellington I Z8964 of 12 OTU Chipping Warden, Northamptonshire hit trees of Friar Park, Henley-on-Thames whilst low flying, the pilot Sgt Carrick F. Lock was showing off to his parents who lived in the town, he flew to low, clipped the tops of the trees and crashed at Cripps Meadow 4th June 1942. He and his three companions including Sgt Duncan D. Dunlop were killed in the crash, Sgt Lock is buried in Holy Trinity Church, Henley, Sgt Dunlop is buried in Benson. **2**

Handley-Page Halifax V DG283 'MA-Y' of 161 Squadron took off from Tempsford, Bedfordshire at 19.57 p.m. and crashed due to engine failure in a field behind the Old Post House near Henley Park, Fawley on 15th March 1943 on an outward journey for operation DIRECTOR 34 heading for France. The aircraft caught fire and most of the injured were pulled clear by F/O Osborn who later received the George Medal, the other crew being Sgt Stevens, F/O D. Thornton, Sgt R Poltock, Sgt Shearer, Sgt B. Crane. **3**

Presentation aircraft, Supermarine Spitfire II P8013 'Burdwan' of 57 OTU Hawarden force-landed in bad weather 1 mile north-east of Henley-on-Thames 21st March 1943 the aircraft was recovered and sent to Air Service Training for repair on the 28th March.

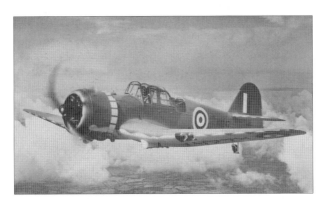

A Miles Master II (Museum of Berkshire Aviation)

An accident involving the Wargrave scoutmaster occurred on the 26th August 1943. Charles Brian Field who was employed by Miles Aircraft at Woodley as a test pilot was doing engine tests in a Miles Master II DM239 when the aircraft broke up in a high-speed dive and crashed at Ashley Hill Wood near Warren Row, Berkshire. His passenger Maurice Cullimore was thrown clear and managed to parachute to safety, Charles Field died in the accident. **4**

Boeing B-17F-30-DL Serial number 42-3171 named 'The Blivit' of the 92nd Bomber Group, based at Podington, Bedfordshire force-landed in a field neighbouring Homestead Cottages at Shiplake Cross, Oxfordshire close to Memorial Avenue on the 14th October 1943. A guard was placed at the entrance to the field. The aircraft was later dismantled and taken away. **5**

Republic P-47C-5-RE Thunderbolt 41-6401 'HV-G' 'Dream Baby' of the 56th Fighter Group, 61st Fighter Squadron at Halesworth, Suffolk crashed 3 miles North-East of Henley-on-Thames due to bad weather on the 31st December 1943, the pilot baled out.
(photo Danny Morris via Peter Randall)

An article in the *Henley Standard* told about an American pilot based in Essex who was romantically linked to a girl who lived in Henley-on-Thames. He would apparently fly over the town in his P-47 Thunderbolt aeroplane with the wheels down, which was a signal to her that he was about to land at the airfield so that she could have a taxi ready and waiting to collect him.

Airspeed Horsa I HG755 assault glider of 1 Heavy Glider Maintenance Unit, Netheravon, Wiltshire was released from the tug aircraft in cloud and stalled during a forced-landing, near Fairmile Cemetery, Henley-on-Thames on the 7th March 1944. **7**

Handley-Page Halifax III LK794 'LK-Q' known as Q-Queenie of 578 Squadron took off from Burn, North Yorkshire at 4.11 a.m., it developed a serious fire close to one of the starboard engines and exploded, it crashed at Applehouse Hill, Carpenters Wood near Burchetts Green, Berkshire on the 18th July 1944 at 5.20 a.m. en route to Caen in Normandy to bomb fortified positions. Of the seven crew on board six died, and one survived, F/Sgt Sloan, the rear gunner, by baling out. The six who died were F/O Victor Starkoff DFC (RAAF), P/O Jan Frederick Fink, F/Sgt Ivor Morgan, P/O Lloyde Hinson Hopper (RCAF), Sgt Gerald Thomas Nicholson and F/Sgt John Edward Claque. **8**

Memorial in Carpenters Wood for the aircrew of Halifax LK794
built by Hugh Cawdron and unveiled on the site in November 2008. (DJP)

The Loss of Boeing B-17 'Sunrise Serenader'

Boeing B-17F-25-BO serial number 41-24575 'SU-J' named 'Sunrise Serenader' of the 384th Bomber Group, 544th Bomber Squadron of the 8th United States Air Force based at Grafton Underwood, Northamptonshire. On the 13th November 1943 the aircraft was on it's way to a raid on Bremen, Germany when at 0919 hours flying at 10,000 feet smoke could be seen coming from one of the port engines. They jettisoned their bombs in Shiplake Meadow. The engine suddenly detached itself from the wing and the aircraft began to vibrate, and went over sharply onto it's left wing and then over onto it's right before rearing up and entering a spin. As the plane levelled out it broke in half and crashed with parts falling into Hennerton backwater and fields by the Sailing Club between Shiplake and Wargrave. The ball turret fell into the river with the operator still inside and was missing for some time. Of the crew of ten nine died in the accident, the sole survivor was T/Sgt Alan Purdy, the radio operator who was seated where the aircraft broke in half. He parachuted safely to the ground and landed in Wargrave Manor. The following aircrew are known to have died in the accident, the Pilot 2nd Lt Ralph J. Connell, the Co-Pilot 2nd Lt Albert M Doman, Navigator 2nd Lt Lawrence M Angthius, Bombardier 2nd Lt Claude I Gober, Engineer T/Sgt Harvey A Wick, Ball Turret Gunner S/Sgt Ellsworth F Calder, and Waist Gunners S/Sgt William M McCully and S/Sgt Kenneth Barr. **6** (With thanks to Jim Waldron)

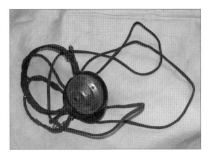

A set of headphones from the crash, they are of a telephone type made in Germany by Personiphone pre 1941.

Boeing B-17F 'Flying Fortress.' (DJP)

T/Sgt Alan B. Purdy.

A piece of the parachute on which Alan Purdy descended to earth from the stricken Bomber.

Jean Purdy the wife of the only survivor of the crash T/Sgt Alan Purdy, visited the village of Wargrave many times during the 1970's. Sadly Alan Purdy died of Cancer in 1979 aged 56. He stayed in the Air Force Reserve after the war and gained the rank of Lieutenant Colonel.

The V rocket believed to be a V2 that is believed to have broke-up in flight came down close to the airfield at 10 a.m. on the 19th March 1945, did not just cause damage to the airfield it also caused damage to the Four Horseshoes Public House, where the stable building had all it's slates blown off the roof. Damage was also sustained by several houses including cottages close by which had to be condemned. Glass from buildings some distance away was shattered, the children in the local school had taken shelter under their desks as the building was shaken, luckily there were no serious casualties. A V2 flies at supersonic speed and on impact buries itself in the ground, the resulting explosion causes most damage by debris flung up into the air from both the crater left by the impact to shrapnel from the rocket and sends a shock wave through the ground, that does the damage to the buildings. **9**

Local Wartime Accidents and Incidents Approximate Locations

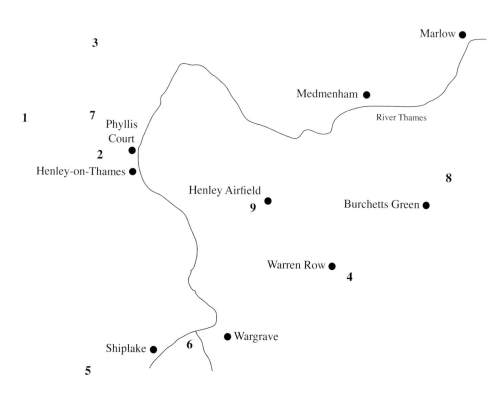

Abbreviations

AA	Anti-Aircraft
AC	Aircraftsman
ACAC	Aircrew Allocation Centre
A/Com	Air Commodore
AFC	Air Force Cross
AFEE	Airborne Forces Experimental Establishment
AFU	Advanced Flying Unit
A.M.	Air Men
AOA	Air Officer in charge of Administration
AOC	Air Officer Commanding
AOP	Air Observation Post
ATA	Air Transport Auxiliary
ATC	Air Training Corps
AVM	Air Vice-Marshal
BC	Bomber Command
BEA	British European Airways
CDO	Civil Defence Officer
CH	Chain Home (radar station)
C-in-C	Commander-in-Chief
CO	Commanding Officer
Cpl	Corporal
DAP	Department of Aircraft Production
DF	Direction Finding
DFC	Distinguished Flying Cross
DH	de Havilland
EFTS	Elementary Flying Training School
ELG	Emergency Landing Ground
E.T.	Early Treatment
FIS	Flying Instructors School
F/Lt	Flight Lieutenant
F/O	Flying Officer
F/Sgt	Flight Sergeant
FTC	Flying Training Command
FTS	Flying Training School
G/Capt	Group Captain
HQ	Headquarters
HQFTC	Headquarters Flying Training Command
IF	Intermediate Frequency
(k)	Killed
LAC	Leading Aircraftsman
LG	Landing Ground
Lt	Lieutenant
MAP	Ministry of Aircraft Production
M.I.	Medical Inspection
M.T.	Motor Transport
MU	Maintenance Unit
NAAFI	Navy, Army and Air Force Institutes
NCO	Non-commissioned Officer
NPL	National Physics Laboratory
NII-VVS	Naoutchno-Ispytatelnyi Institut Voenno Vozdouchnyi Sil (Research Institute of the Soviet Air Force)
OAE	Otdelnaya Aviatsyonnaya Eskadrilya (Independent Reconnaissance Squadron)
O/C	Officer Commanding
ORAP	Otdelnyj Razvedyvatelnyj Aviatsionnyj Polk (Independent Recce Aviation Regiment)
ORB	Operations Record Book

OTU	Operational Training Unit
PDC	Personnel Despatch Centre
PDRC	Personnel Despatch and Reception Centre
P/O	Pilot Officer
PMO	Principal Medical Officer
PoW	Prisoner of War
RAE	Royal Aircraft Establishment
RAFO	Royal Air Force Officer
RAFVR	Royal Air Force Volunteer Reserve
RCAF	Royal Canadian Air Force
RLG	Relief Landing Ground
RNAS	Royal Naval Air Station
RNVR	Royal Naval Volunteer Reserve
RNZAF	Royal New Zealand Air Force
SAAF	South African Air Force
Sgt	Sergeant
S/Sgt	Staff Sergeant
T/Sgt	Technical Sergeant
S/L	Squadron Leader
SOE	Special Operations Executive
Sqn	Squadron
TRE	Telecommunications Research Establishment
USAAF	United States Army Air Force
USCG	United States Coast Guard
VE	Victory in Europe
VHF	Very High Frequency
WAAF	Women's Auxiliary Air Force
W/Cdr	Wing Commander
W/O	Warrant Officer

Previously Published by the Author

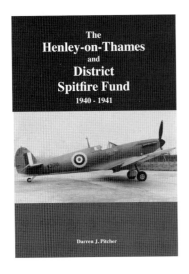

The Henley-on-Thames and District Spitfire Fund 1940-1941
Published by Robert Boyd Publications
ISBN: 978 1 89953688 7

Records the town of Henley-on-Thames efforts to raise the £5,000 required to buy a Spitfire, includes all the fund raising details of the events organised by the towns-folk and lists all the individual names of the donators and donation amounts. Also included is the full history of the actual Spitfire including operations flown and pilot names and hours flown. Published August 2008 and available from the authors address shown at the front of this book. 48 pages. Price £5.99